CLASSIC
NORDIC
Recipes

Berit Öström

Berit Öström

is a native of Stockholm, Sweden, but has called Melbourne, Australia — where she has had a successful career in publishing and marketing — home for a very long time. Her love for the traditional Swedish food of her childhood has never waned. To her delight this food is still as popular as ever and regularly served in Swedish homes, schools, restaurants and cafés.

These traditional dishes, along with the cuisines of all Scandinavian countries, have stood the test of time and their simplicity, few ingredients and reliance on local seasonal produce are the precursors to the New Nordic Diet, now recognised as one of the healthiest diets in the world.

Continuing the Swedish food culture is important to Berit and she has never stopped cooking dishes as "in the old country" for her family and friends "in the new country".

WP

Published by:
Wilkinson Publishing Pty Ltd
ACN 006 042 173
Level 4, 2 Collins St Melbourne,
Victoria, Australia 3000
Ph: +61 3 9654 5446
www.wilkinsonpublishing.com.au

International distribution by Pineapple Media Limited
(wwwpineapple-media.com)   ISSN 2200-0151

National Library of Australia Cataloguing-in-Publication entry:

Creator:	Öström, Berit, author.
Title:	Classic Nordic recipes : simple, seasonal meals the Swedish way / Berit Öström.
ISBN:	9781925265408 (paperback)
Subjects:	Cooking, Scandinavian. Cooking.
Dewey Number:	641.5948
Layout Design:	Corinda Cook, Tango Media Pty Ltd
Cover Design:	Alicia Freile, Tango Media Pty Ltd

Recipe images by agreement with Berit Öström, all other images by agreement with iStock/Getty.

CONTENTS

AUTHOR'S NOTE

If there's only one thing I can say about this book, it is that it's authentic. All recipes are as they were when I was a child and still lived in Stockholm, Sweden. Now that I have a family of my own and live in Melbourne, Australia, these traditional dishes are regulars on our dinner table. Food is like language – it is forever evolving and blending with influences from around the world. Take the famous *gravlax* for example – as a preserved food staple it goes back several hundred years, yet today the recipe for this essentially very simple dish has been recreated by some of the world's most famous chefs . . . there's Mediterranean gravlax, Middle Eastern gravlax, there's even an Asian-flavoured gravlax.

Generally, traditional Nordic recipes are a case study in simplicity – few and local ingredients, seasonal produce and uncomplicated seasoning.

This is how the best food comes together, flavours come to the fore with nowhere to hide.

Another aspect of this publication is that all photographs are genuinely unadulterated – they have all been taken by me and my daughter-in-law Kerryn Martinsen. There are no glazes, no enhancements, no tricks whatsoever – the food in the photograph is exactly as I have prepared it. And consequently of course, close to what each dish will look like when you cook it yourself!

I really hope you will like the authenticity of the dishes, recipes and photography – and of course that many of the dishes will become regular fare on your dinner table, whether for every day or celebratory occasions.

All the best
Berit Öström

THE NORDIC CUISINE
AND THE
NORDIC DIET

There is a lot of interest, as well as research, into what is generally known as the Nordic Diet. It has been compared to the Mediterranean Diet for its health properties and recognised as a healthy diet better suited to a colder, northern climate. What is not necessarily widely understood however is that comparison is based on the principles of the New Nordic Cuisine rather than the Traditional Nordic Diet. So what exactly are the similarities and differences?

The similarities are the same for all three concepts – local seasonal ingredients, fatty fish (such as salmon, herring, mackerel and trout), cabbage, root vegetables, berries, herbs, apples, pears and whole grains. The main difference between the Nordic Diet and the Traditional Nordic Diet is that the first incorporates all the foods of the second, but with less dairy and sugar and increased intake of fish.

The New Nordic Cuisine is also based on the same principles, but with a wider and even more localised selection of ingredients, more emphasis on food grown in the wild, more fish and game, and very low amounts of sugar and dairy.

This food philosophy came out of the frustration that the co-owner of the now world-famous restaurant Noma in Copenhagen, Claus Meyer, had with bland Danish food.

In the autumn of 2004, he brought together the greatest regional Scandinavian chefs for a Nordic Cuisine Symposium where they formulated the principles of the New Nordic Kitchen Manifesto. The following year, the Nordic Council of Ministers adopted the manifesto as the ideology of a New Nordic Food program. The Manifesto also became a roadmap for food growers and manufacturers to care about the quality, sustainability and nutrition of what they produce.

At the core of the New Nordic Kitchen Manifesto was the belief that Scandinavian foods should be healthy, seasonal and varied, based on locally grown, organic, nutrient-dense ingredients and importantly for the more visionary chefs, innovative without losing its traditional core. Naturally, the restaurant Noma is one of the main driving forces behind the interest and popularity of the Nordic Diet and we owe a lot to these dedicated individuals for the recognition of Nordic foods as a healthy and nutritious diet.

To get a real feel for what Claus Meyer set out to achieve with the Manifesto, the following is the content outline as displayed on Meyer's website www.clausmeyer.dk. In true Scandinavian minimalistic style, it consists of a brief introduction followed by ten succinct points.

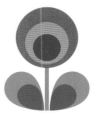

As Nordic chefs we find that the time has now come for us to create a New Nordic Kitchen, which in virtue of its good taste and special character compares favourable [sic] with the standard of the greatest kitchens of the world.

THE AIMS OF NEW NORDIC CUISINE ARE

1. To express the purity, freshness, simplicity and ethics we wish to associate with our region.
2. To reflect the changing of the seasons in the meals we make.
3. To base our cooking on ingredients and produce whose characteristics are particularly excellent in our climates, landscapes and waters.
4. To combine the demand for good taste with modern knowledge of health and well-being.
5. To promote Nordic products and the variety of Nordic producers – and to spread the word about their underlying cultures.
6. To promote animal welfare and a sound production process in our seas, on our farmland and in the wild.
7. To develop potentially new applications of traditional Nordic food products.
8. To combine the best in Nordic cookery and culinary traditions with impulses from abroad.
9. To combine local self-sufficiency with regional sharing of high-quality products.
10. To join forces with consumer representatives, other cooking craftsmen, agriculture, the fishing, food, retail and wholesale industries, researchers, teachers, politicians and authorities on this project for the benefit and advantage of everyone in the Nordic countries.

The Traditional Nordic Diet

is rich in plant foods, root vegetables, cabbage, berries, fatty fish, apples, pears and whole grains, especially rye. Herbs and spices also feature heavily in Swedish cooking – chives, thyme, fennel, cardamom, juniper berries and parsley, to name the most popular. However, the king of herbs is dill – it is used in almost every dish involving fish or seafood, as well as a flavouring in pickled herring, dips, chips and even crisp bread.

The oil of choice is canola oil, especially the virgin cold-pressed variety – often referred to as 'the olive oil of the north'. Canola oil is very versatile as it can be used for baking and frying and is also suited to make mayonnaise, dressings and marinades. The cold-pressed oil contains the healthy fatty acids omega 3, 6 and 9 and is a natural source of vitamin E.

Nordic food is about simplicity, where the main ingredient, whether fish, vegetables or meat, is what flavours the dish, thus remaining pure and with few additional ingredients. Generally it is cooked from scratch – and this is still the case in many homes in Sweden. The introduction of fast-food outlets has not changed this to as great a degree as in many other Western cultures – cooking a meal at home for the family is still the norm today.

The Nordic Diet is recognised for its health properties – but an interesting aspect of the Traditional Nordic Diet is that when you examine each recipe, you find some contain a healthy amount of sugar, salt and/or cream. And yet, when you eat the whole spectrum of dishes, they complement one another both nutrition and calorie-wise, which is one of the reasons Scandinavians are among the slimmest in the world.

I have not shied away from keeping the traditional recipes intact – the way my grandmother and my parents cooked for their families and the way I do for mine. I have included the most popular dishes that have stood the test of time. You can of course change cream for milk, or use margarine instead of butter, reduce the amount of salt or sugar, but for that authentic Swedish taste I would hope you try it at least once before amending, and hopefully love it so much you stay with the traditional version.

You can also rest assured that all ingredients required for these recipes are readily available in Australia, Europe and North America – or, as in the recipe for Marinated Smoked Trout, it has been modified to include produce accessible in these regions. Unfortunately, some traditional dishes rely on produce either too difficult to obtain outside Sweden or Scandinavia, and no comparable substitute is readily available.

So let's review some of the ingredients used in the recipes in this publication from a nutritional and health benefit perspective (without getting too technical) – and it turns out they're pretty impressive . . .

BERRIES

All berries are low in calories, full of antioxidants and vitamins,

yet there are differences between one fruit and another.

Lingonberries – also known as cowberries or foxberries they're packed with antioxidants and research shows that the lingonberry has higher concentrations of plant polyphenol flavonoids than any other type of berry. So what does this mean? Well it means that lingonberries not only strengthen your wellbeing via their antioxidants, they also assist your body to replace depleted antioxidants – especially the kind known as 'master antioxidants' because they help fight off almost every illness.

Blueberries – long ignored by health professionals due to their relatively low Vitamin C content compared to other berries such as strawberries, it is now universally accepted that the blueberry is a nutritional powerhouse. More than any berry, blueberries are super-loaded with nutritional and powerful antioxidants. Studies show that a diet that includes daily intake of blueberries can improve and maintain eye health, regulate blood sugar, improve motor skills

and reverse short-term memory loss, as well as help reduce the risk for infections.

The bilberry, which grows wild in northern Europe is a flatter and more acidic variety – but with the benefit that it grows prolifically close to urban areas. Picking blueberries, and lingonberries for that matter, is still a weekend pursuit in late summer/early autumn for many Swedish families.

Strawberries – one serve (about 8-10 berries) of this beautiful red berry contains 85mg of Vitamin C, which is calculated at 160% of the recommended daily value. That's more Vitamin C than in an orange! Research has confirmed that eating one or two servings of strawberries a day may help improve heart health, lower blood pressure and also help in the prevention of some cancers.

Raspberries – these sweet and brightly coloured berries are low in calories and fat, cholesterol-free and high in fibre, Vitamin C and antioxidants. Daily intake of one or two servings of raspberries will support heart health.

FISH

Fatty fish such as salmon, mackerel, herring, sardines, trout and eel contain significant amounts of oil throughout the body tissue as well as in the belly cavity. The good news is that all these fish retain the omega-3 fatty acids, regardless of whether they are canned, fresh or frozen.

It is the richness in omega-3 polyunsaturated fatty acids and the lean protein in fatty fish that make eating these fish so healthy. Research has shown that regularly eating oily fish can reduce the risk of cardiovascular disease, improve mental ability, ward off cancer, and lower the risk of rheumatoid arthritis.

HERBS

Herbs are a given in any kitchen – their smell, aroma, and flavour – and are one of the most enjoyable aspects of cooking. Herbs contain fibre, antioxidants, essential oils, vitamins and many other nutrients that contribute to our wellbeing.

Chives are very low in calories; 100g of fresh chives provides just 30 calories. Nonetheless, they contain many noteworthy flavonoid antioxidants, plant fibre, minerals, and vitamins that have proven health benefits.

Dill, the most popular and prevalent herb in Swedish cuisine, contains no cholesterol and is low in calories. It boasts many antioxidants, vitamins like niacin, pyridoxine etc, and dietary fibre, which help control blood cholesterol levels.

Parsley is another low calorie herb - 100g of fresh leaves is only 36 calories. Its leaves contain no cholesterol or fat but are rich in antioxidants, vitamins, minerals, and dietary fibre. Parsley can help control blood cholesterol, as well as offer protection from free radicals.

Thyme is packed with minerals and vitamins essential for optimum health. Its leaves are one of the richest sources of potassium, iron, calcium, manganese, magnesium, and selenium. Potassium helps control heart rate and blood pressure, whereas iron is crucial for the formation of red blood cells.

Fennel seeds have many health-benefiting nutrients, essential compounds, antioxidants, dietary fibre, minerals, and vitamins. Fennel seeds provide minerals like iron, zinc, selenium and calcium to the body, all very effective in maintaining the oxygen balance. They are also naturally antiseptic.

Cardamom – The cardamom seeds contain a variety of minerals such as calcium, sulphur and phosphorus. They also contain a volatile oil which makes up about 5% of the seed's mass, and have aromatic and medicinal properties. This volatile oil in the cardamom seed has been proven to be a soothing solution for a host of digestive problems.

Juniper berries are actually not berries at all. Rather they are tiny pine cones from the juniper bush, which is why they carry a piney flavour. Some of the health benefits of the juniper berries include acting as antioxidants and anti-bacterial for bacteria-related conditions because of their high levels of unsaturated fats and antioxidants.

ROOT VEGETABLES

Root vegetables, as indicated by their collective name, grow underneath the ground and consequently can absorb high amounts of minerals and other nutrients from the soil. This ability coupled with the ability of the above ground leaves to absorb nutrients from the sun is what makes root vegetables a virtual power-house of top-to-bottom nutrition.

Most root vegetables are high in complex carbohydrates, high in fibre and phytonutrients, and are low in fat as well as calories. Additionally, they are generally high in vitamin C, beta-carotene, and contain essential minerals such as potassium, phosphorous, magnesium and small amounts of iron.

Carrots, sweet potatoes, swede and turnips are particularly high in Vitamin C and beta-carotene, which helps clean the blood and combat high blood pressure, heart disease and stroke.

Cabbage is part of the cruciferous vegetable family, which also includes kale, broccoli, Brussels sprouts and cauliflower, all of which are chock-full of beneficial nutrients. High fibre content, antioxidants, cholesterol-lowering abilities, and sulphur-based compounds all combine to make cabbage and the whole cruciferous family a must inclusion in a healthy diet regime. Interestingly, red cabbage tends to contain more of these compounds than green cabbage.

WHOLE GRAINS

Rye is rich in magnesium, B vitamins, iron, zinc, antioxidants and phytochemicals. It is also very filling due to its water-binding capacity (which can be very beneficial if you are trying to lose weight), which promotes a healthy bowel and helps to manage blood sugars as well as cholesterol levels. Rye bread also contains around three times more fibre than white bread.

Although **oats** are hulled after the roasting process, the hulling does not strip away the bran and germ and thus remain a concentrated source of fibre and nutrients. It is the high antioxidants unique to oats that assist in reducing blood pressure. Oats, oat bran, and oatmeal contain a fibre known as *beta-glucan*, which studies going back 50 years have proven help in lowering cholesterol levels.

Barley is another great source of dietary fibre, both soluble and insoluble. Barley also contains several vitamins and minerals including Vitamin B1 and B3, selenium, iron, magnesium, zinc, phosphorus and copper, as well as antioxidants.

A BRIEF HISTORY OF SWEDISH FOOD & CULTURAL TRADITIONS

Is there really such a thing as genuine Nordic food? Today, as around the world, food served in Scandinavian homes and restaurants often has the flavour of foreign cuisines such as Greek, Italian or Asian.

Yet, Sweden does indeed have a fine old culinary tradition rich in native dishes. The Swedish *husmanskost*, good old everyday Swedish food based on local and seasonal produce cooked very simply, has no doubt been influenced by foreign cuisines over the years – but luckily much remains genuinely Swedish.

The simple and hearty *husmanskost* dishes are still popular, although many of the old recipes have been revised to make them less sturdy, faster to prepare and better suited to the modern way of life. Their special charm, characteristics and flavour however have not been lost in that translation.

SWEDISH LANDSCAPE, FAUNA AND FLORA

Sweden enjoys a long coastline, has large forests and many, many lakes. It is also sparsely populated with most inhabitants living in the southern part of the country. There are extreme weather contrasts between the long summer days and the equally long winter nights.

Its fauna and flora vary from the north to the south – bears and wolves up north and deer and wild boar down south. The many rivers and lakes are hosts to a plethora of aquatic life – such as salmon, pike, perch and signal crayfish, and the Baltic Sea and Atlantic Sea are home to various kinds of herring, cod and mackerel. Prawns and crayfish are fished on the east coast.

Sweden still has virgin forests, wetlands, and unregulated rivers. It also has some 100,000 lakes ranging from clear mountain lakes to forest lakes and nutrient-rich lakes on the flat agricultural plains. It also has just on 700 rivers and streams.

Sweden has two distinct different forests – the coniferous pine and spruce forests and large deciduous tree forests such as birch and aspen. The latter forest is light and sunny with grass and flowers growing under the canopies, whereas the coniferous forests are quiet, dark and mysterious . . . where elves, trolls and other mysterious creatures were believed to flourish . . . as in many Brother Grimms' fairy tales.

Sweden was the first European country to establish a national park back in 1910 – primarily in the mountainous areas of the north. The Right of Public Access also entitles anyone to venture through forests and fields and pick whatever grows wild, such as berries and mushrooms, without asking the landowner's permission.

It is these geographical characteristics that lay the ground for the way the Swedes live, eat and celebrate old and new traditions. They also like structure and order which no doubt contributes to their eagerness to protect their beloved traditions – as well as resisting the temptation to modernise them! It is very comforting to know that when visiting our home country (always in summer), Midsummer Eve will be celebrated the same way it was when we lived there some 40 years ago.

Our family still gathers blueberries, lingonberries and mushrooms – especially the prized chanterelle – just a short drive from inner city Stockholm. The mellow, beautiful and delicious chanterelle mushrooms grow prolifically in the mossy coniferous forests and the most popular way to serve this delicacy is fried in butter on toast and with a sprinkling of a sharp grated cheese on top . . . a true culinary delicacy! Chanterelles are also among the richest known sources of Vitamin D and are very high in potassium.

The following is based on the writings of Professor Jan-Öjvind Swahn, ethnologist, who has written numerous publications on the history, food and traditions of Sweden.

❀   ❀   ❀

As recently as the early 1900s most Swedes still lived in the countryside and lived on what the farm could produce – grain, potatoes, root vegetables, pork, butter and cheese. Sweden being such a long country means the climatic and environmental conditions vary greatly between the north and the south. The northern regions mainly consist of tundra where reindeer herds graze on the mountains and the southern regions where growing and husbandry conditions more resemble those of England or Germany. Each region, relying on whatever ingredients were available locally, developed their own unique dishes – thus, still today, there are distinct differences how some foods are served up north, down south or inbetween.

One good example of this is *bread* – the three kinds of bread you find in Swedish supermarkets are flat bread, crisp bread and various kinds of soft loaves. Due to climatic conditions, barley was the only form of cereal able to be grown in three-quarters of the north of the country. However, barley is very low in gluten and thus not particularly suitable for baking leavened bread. Consequently the barley flour was used to make a thin, unleavened cake either crisp or soft and which could even be cooked on a heated hearth.

South of the barley belt, rye would grow, harvested and milled into rye flour – excellent flour for baking loaves of bread. However, keeping the flour fresh, free of mildew and away from rodents proved a problem and the only lasting solution was to convert the flour into bread without haste. Essential to this concept was to produce a bread that would not go mouldy, nor become inedible when dried out. And so was invented the kind of Swedish bread that is now eaten and available all around the world – the humble crisp bread. Brittle little flat cakes of rye full of fibre and delicious with just about any topping you can imagine.

Once the windmill was introduced, flour could be ground on demand, and thus fresh, soft bread could be baked every day. The initial impact of the windmills was confined to the capital Stockholm and other urban cities further south.

To this day, regional traditions remain – bakery statistics show very clearly that the old regional patterns of the old subsistence economy: far more soft loaves are consumed in the south as well in the cities and far more flat bread in the north and far more crisp bread in between.

One of the most recognisable fish dishes from Sweden is *gravlax* – now served the world over, every self-respecting chef seems to have their own take on this culinary delight.

In its traditional form, the curing only uses four ingredients – sugar, salt, dill and white pepper. Some regional recipes also add juniper berries. Over time and experimentation, additional ingredients such as beetroot, horseradish, mustard seeds, fennel and alcohol have been added to the basic recipe.

Gravlax is a dish with a long history and has been prepared and eaten in the north of Sweden since the 14th Century. The word 'grav' means grave and 'lax' is simply salmon in Swedish. The original and primitive version of gravlax got its name from the fact it was buried soon after catching. Salt was also a very expensive commodity, prohibiting the option of proper salting. The fisherman dug a deep trench, lined it with birch bark and placed the fish in it, along with sufficient salt to ensure it fermented instead of rotting. The reason for this process was that the fishing places along the rivers where salm-on were making their way upriver in spring to spawn, were a long way away from the farms. No roads, plenty of water-logged earth would make the rivers inaccessible by cart – until autumn when it was again possible to travel with a cart or sled and retrieve the fermented salmon... which was actually called 'surlaks' (sour salmon) in the old days.

Gravlax is a good example of how survival in a harsh climate necessitated clever and innovative thinking – and created foods that have not only survived but thrived to today.

Some food traditions that have also stood the test of time are 'bruna bönor och fläsk' (brown beans and salted pork) on Tuesdays, pea soup and pork on Thursdays and fish on Fridays are still served on their allocated days. The Thursday pea soup tradition goes back to the Middle Ages when Swedes were still Catholics, as Friday was a fast day the habit of eating boiled dried peas to fill up before fast began. By the time Swedes turned Lutheran in the 16th Century, pea soup on Thursday was ingrained in the Swedish psyche. Over time pea soup has become a little more luxurious by the addition of pickled pork and accompanied by 'punch', an alcoholic arrak-flavoured beverage that is drunk hot.

Another fascinating tradition is the feast each August where *crayfish* (kräftor in Swedish) are consumed ceremoniously by the light of paper lanterns while wearing silly hats and bibs – and preferably under a full moon. The crayfish are cooked in brine with lots of dill crowns, and there is a lot of singing for each 'snaps' toast – there are hundreds of different songs to accompany each 'skål' and bottom up. The crayfish party (kräftskiva) with its ceremonial and traditional progression is something that must be experienced to be truly appreciated.

❀ ❀ ❀

FIKA – MUCH MORE THAN HAVING A COFFEE

One of the first words you'll hear when visiting Sweden is *fika*. The word is becoming more known with many Swedish Cafes around the world naming their establishment Fika, for example Fika in New York. Maybe before long it will be as recognised as *smörgåsbord*, *gravlax* or *ombudsman*. The Swedes, being wedded to their traditions, are reluctant to translate the word *fika* and risk it losing its true meaning and becoming a mere coffee break.

To the Swedes, *fika* is not so much about the coffee as it is a cherished and legitimate reason to spend some quality time with friends, family or colleagues. You can *fika* any time, it is not restricted to any one time-slot or event, and can be enjoyed at home, at work, in a café or anywhere else people gather. It can be a little overwhelming for the first-time visitor as it is a tradition carried out several times a day. And if you were to politely say 'no thank you' to a *fika*, you are likely to be met by disbelief and even incredulity ... what? You don't want (yet another) *fika*?

As much as the concept of a 'slät' cup of coffee (i.e. a cup of coffee without accompanying sweets) does exist, this is actually not regarded as a *fika* per se, as accompanying sweets are crucial to the concept. It matters little whether the sweets are cinnamon buns, cakes or even savoury open sandwiches – they are all accepted as true *fika* fare. Given this enduring and much-loved tradition it is no surprise to find that Swedes are the top consumers of coffee in the world – not to mention sugar!

THE SMÖRGÅSBORD

The Swedish smörgåsbord is well known throughout the world and is always served in most Swedish homes at special events such as Christmas, Easter and Midsummer. It is also the mainstay of food to celebrate a special milestone, such as a 50th birthday, graduation or engagement.

To the uninitiated it can be confusing as to how to approach the plethora of dishes on the smörgåsbord and not end up with a plate that's a hotchpotch of flavours and impressions. Luckily there are rules on how to approach the smörgåsbord – and rule No 1 is to not try to sample everything at once.

The convention is to change to a clean plate between each serving.

Start with the pickled herring, accompanied by potato, egg halves, crisp bread, cheese and if to your taste sour cream with chives, dill, or red onions. Second comes the other fish dishes – gravlax, hot or cold smoked salmon, poached or grilled fish; along with the suitable condiments. Once you've relished this offering, help yourself to the cold meat cuts and salads, followed by the hot dishes such as meatballs, roast beef and sausages.

The traditional beverage is beer, along with a 'snaps', or schnapps, served with the first course, i.e. the pickled herring. Singing is optional – although it has to be said there are few occasions more suitable for a bit of sing along as when downing a 'snaps'.

THE SWEDISH OPEN SANDWICH

Open sandwiches are very popular in Scandinavia, especially in Sweden and Denmark, but for several hundred years it was only farmers who ate open sandwiches.

Open sandwiches were practical for the farmers to bring into the field. The combination of solid wholegrain bread topped with leftovers was very filling and practical, and the thick slice of rye bread served as a plate, so lunch could be eaten without plates or cutlery.

For breakfast, the bread – rye bread and crisp bread mostly – is served with an array of sandwich meat, cheese, pâté and sliced cucumber, capsicum and tomato. Each person makes their own sandwich with their preferred topping and eats it whole out of the hand.

For lunch or with 'fika', a more elaborate version is often served, where the prawn sandwich reigns supreme – white bread topped with lettuce, egg slices, mayonnaise and prawns, and decorated with lemon, cucumber, tomato and dill – a very colourful and pretty sandwich indeed.

The second favourite open sandwich is meatballs with beetroot salad, with garnish such as tomato, cucumber, sliced orange and parsley adding to the colourful presentation. These elaborate open sandwiches would be impossible to consume without the 'aid' of a knife and fork, so no hand-holding is required!

If smaller sized open sandwiches are served as an entrée, they are also eaten with a knife and fork. The toppings are also adjusted to season and occasion but always follow the smörgåsbord principle, i.e. one sandwich with fish or seafood, one with meat and one with cheese. The bread is almost always of a dark variety such as wholemeal, dark rye or if white bread is used it is generally of the sourdough variety. As an aside, it is handy to know that Swedes often serve bread, butter and cheese with every meal – each person makes their own open sandwich which is eaten whole! The etiquette of breaking the bread and eating it piece by piece does not apply – the bread is eaten straight out of the hand.

CHRISTMAS

Slaughtering, beer brewing, cooking, baking, candle making – these were some of the holiday preparations common in the old farming household. Today most Swedes lead a comfortable urban life and practically the entire Christmas holiday fare may be bought ready-made.

Nevertheless, come December the smell of cinnamon and saffron, candles, copper polish and the occasional wet wool smell will be noticed in Swedish homes. At no other time of the year do Swedes take so much care in preserving old customs as at *jul* and doing your own cooking and baking is part of the Christmas tradition.

The all-important day of celebration, feasting and gift giving is *julafton*, Christmas Eve and festivities usually start with a Christmas smörgåsbord early in the afternoon. All the traditional dishes are served – pickled herring, meatballs, spare ribs, herring salad and of course the traditional Christmas ham. The ham has been pickled then soaked, boiled and lastly covered in a mustard and egg mixture and browned in the oven.

EASTER

Easter signifies the early signs of spring – it means sunshine, snow, skiing, tulips, daffodils and budding birch twigs adorned with multi-coloured feathers. Easter is also when young girls dress as witches, a reminder of earlier times when Easter was marked by a strong belief in dark forces and super-stition. In the old days, Easter week even had its own menu that included kale soup, salt salmon pudding and boiled coloured eggs among other dishes.

Today, there are no particular set rules, but depending on when Easter falls, the first 'primör', or new season vegetables along with pickled or oven baked salmon, or a pork or lamb roast preceded by a vegetable soup often take pride of place on the dinner table.

MIDSUMMER

This is the time of year when it seems like the sun never sets. In fact, in the north of Sweden it doesn't, and in the south only for an hour or two. This calls for celebration! Friends and family gather for the most typical Swedish tradition of all: Midsummer.

Midsummer is a joyous celebration of summer, sunshine, youth and love. It is also an occasion that carries with it a lot of nostalgia. Deep inside, Swedes agree on what Midsummer is, how to celebrate it and how it should proceed. To celebrate Midsummer by an inland lake or an inlet in the archipelago is to be not just truly privileged – it is a must! Water and Midsummer celebrations go hand-in-hand.

All over Sweden people gather to dance around the 'midsommarstång', the Maypole, covered in wild flowers, birch twigs and bright coloured ribbons while singing songs that go back centuries or more. A wreath of flowers worn throughout the day and night is another tradition that is still as strong as ever. And very pretty too!

An amazing number of people still dress up in the traditional dress of their district - there's even a Sweden dress, always worn by the Queen and Princesses at Midsummer. This is the time when you stay up all night to watch the sun never go down past the horizon – and the further north you are the higher the sun remains in the sky throughout the night. Many young girls also pick seven different flowers to put under the pillow to 'dream about their future husband', one of the many old and still living traditions.

THE MIDSUMMER SMÖRGÅSBORD

A typical Midsummer smörgåsbord menu features several kinds of pickled herring, boiled new potatoes with fresh dill, sour cream and chives, followed by baked, cured or hot smoked salmon and some kind of grilled meat. There is only one dessert worthy of the midsummer smörgåsbord and that is strawberry and cream cake – moist sponge cake filled with strawberry jam and custard and decorated with cream and lots, and lots of strawberries.

The traditional accompaniment is a cold beer and schnapps, preferably spiced – wine just does not go well with this kind of food.

KRÄFTSKIVA – CRAYFISH PARTY

As far back as the 1500s, the bright red crayfish have been eaten in Sweden, although it was only the aristocracy who enjoyed these delicacies in those days.

Fast forward to the mid-1800s and people started eating crayfish as they are eaten today. This is when the crayfish party, or *kräftskiva* as it is known in Swedish, held in the month of August spread through the middle classes. By the 1900s, crayfish was entrenched in the Swedish cuisine as a national delicacy and eating the crustaceans became an annual event to say goodbye to summer and welcome autumn – and August was also the time when the crayfish was ready to be fished.

The crayfish party follows a rather strict ceremonial process – there are traditional accompaniments to be served with the crayfish, all participants wear hats and bibs, there's schnapps of course and there's singing, lots and lots of singing!

STARTERS & APPETISERS

Pickled Herring
Inlagd sill

Swedes love pickled herring and not one single festive occasion is complete without it. Pickled herring comes in many flavours and varieties, but this recipe is the most traditional, combining spices, onion and carrot to make a relatively mild, yet tasty, pickled herring. As with all pickled herring, it is served with boiled potatoes, hard-boiled egg halves, sour cream and chopped chives, along with crisp bread and a hard cheese.

SERVES 4–6

6-8 pre-soaked herring fillets

350ml (1 ½ cups) water

220g (1 cup) caster sugar

250ml (1 cup) white vinegar

2 tsp whole allspice, crushed

2 tsp yellow mustard seeds

4 tsp whole white peppercorns

1 red/Spanish onion, sliced into rings

2 carrots, sliced into thin discs

2 handfuls of fresh dill

2 bay leaves

Cut the herring fillets crosswise into approximately 3cm/1 inch strips.

In a stainless steel saucepan, combine the water, sugar, vinegar, allspice, mustard seeds and peppercorns. Bring the pickling liquid to the boil, stirring to dissolve the sugar. Remove from the heat and set aside to cool completely.

Arrange the herring fillets, onion, carrots, dill and bay leaves in a glass serving dish. Pour the cold pickling liquid over the herring, ensuring all ingredients are covered. Cover with cling wrap and refrigerate overnight or for up to 2 days before serving.

Serve with boiled potatoes, hard-boiled eggs, sour cream and a healthy amount of chopped chives and dill, along with crisp bread and cheese. Or top a piece of crisp bread with cold mashed potatoes, hard-boiled egg slices, pickled herring and garnish with red onion rings, crushed all spice and dill sprigs.

Toast Skagen
Toast Skagen

Toast Skagen is probably the most-loved starter in Sweden and has stood the test of time and influences by international cuisines and trends du jour. It's simple yet complex in flavour, but it does rely on quality prawns — super fresh and bursting with flavour. There is something magical about the relationship between the butter-fried white bread and the Skagen mix that cannot be experienced by using plain toast — so indulge yourself and enjoy the taste sensation!

SERVES 6

500g/1 lb fresh prawns, unpeeled, or 400g/14 oz peeled (*)

1 small red/Spanish onion

1 bunch of dill

50ml (¼ cup) egg mayonnaise

50ml (¼ cup) crème fraîche or sour cream

1 tbsp lemon juice

Zest of one lemon

Salt and white pepper

6 white square loaf slices

Red-gold caviar (optional)

(*) If fresh prawns are no available, use the best quality frozen prawns you can find

Peel and chop the prawns coarsely, and chop the dill and the red onion very finely. Mix the mayonnaise, crème fraîche, chopped dill and onion, lemon juice and finely grated lemon zest together then add the prawns. Add salt and pepper to taste – the saltiness of the prawns will determine how much you need.

Cut the bread slices into rounds and fry in butter until golden, set aside until cool. Top with the Skagen mix and garnish with a dill sprig and lemon, and caviar if using.

Marinated hot smoked rainbow trout
Marinerad rökt regnbågsforell

My second favourite entrée (after Toast Skagen) is this simple, yet so satisfying dish. The Swedish version uses 'böckling', a smoked Baltic herring, also known as buckling in English. As buckling is not easily found outside Sweden I use smoked rainbow trout instead in this recipe — it is not as robust in flavour as the buckling, but works beautifully nevertheless. One taste sensation I really like about this dish is that the marinade makes the dill go really crispy and enhances the aroma.

SERVES 4-6

1 whole hot smoked rainbow trout

25g (½ cup) dill sprigs

6 tbsp canola or virgin olive oil

3 tbsp white or apple cider vinegar

1 tsp freshly ground white pepper

1 tbsp sweet Swedish mustard (or 1 tbsp Dijon mustard and ¼ tsp caster sugar)

Salt to taste

Clean the trout, remove the skin and all bones, then flake and put aside.

Mix oil, vinegar, pepper and mustard (and sugar if using) – taste the marinade and adjust seasoning as required. The marinade should be tasty, but not so strong it overpowers the delicate flavour of the trout.

Put the smoked trout flakes on a shallow dish, cover with the dill sprigs, then pour over the marinade. Leave to infuse for at least two hours before serving.

Serve with toast or plain crackers and extra cracked white pepper.

THE SWEDISH SANDWICH CAKE

Behold the Swedish sandwich cake . . . the 'smörgåstårta' is a guaranteed success at any celebration in Swedish society – this culinary delight is a given on the smörgåsbord, but is also served as a light lunch dish, or even as a classy entrée. There is an abundance of variations on the core theme of bread layered with creamy fillings and creatively decorated to tempt and impress both the eye and the taste buds. The seafood sandwich cake is the most prized, but we also bring you a ham and paté torte, as well as a vegetarian one. Whichever you choose, it will be the talking point of your party.

Interestingly, the concept of a cake made from savoury ingredients is a relative newcomer to the Swedish cuisine. It was created by a pastry chef in northern Sweden in 1966 but it was during the 1970s that it really made it onto the smörgåsbord – especially at celebrations of milestone life events such as engagements, 50th birthdays and the like.

Seafood sandwich cake

Smörgåstårta med skaldjur

SERVES 12-14

12 slices white bread,
cut lengthwise (*)

**FIRST AND THIRD
LAYER FILLING**

1 large can of tuna in spring
water

150ml (½ cup plus 1 tbsp)
mayonnaise

200ml (¾ cup plus 1 tbsp)
crème fraîche

1 small red/Spanish onion,
finely chopped

SECOND LAYER FILLING

3 hard-boiled eggs

Dill sprigs

400g/14 oz smoked trout
mousse

GARNISH

150ml (½ cup plus 1 tbsp)
mayonnaise

50ml (¼ cup) crème fraîche

Lettuce

TOPPING/DECORATIONS

10 slices smoked salmon

500g/1 lb prawns, peeled

4 hard-boiled eggs

Tomatoes

Cucumber

Dill sprigs

Lemon slices, or wedges

(*) Ask your baker to cut the
bread lengthwise, instead
of the standard sandwich size.

Prepare the bread: Remove the crusts from all slices and butter 9 slices, leaving 3 slices unbuttered. Buttering the bread helps 'stabilise' the cake and counteracts the potential for the bread to go 'mushy'.

First and third layer filling: Drain the tuna and break up into smaller flakes. Mix the tuna with the mayonnaise, crème fraîche and chopped red onion. Taste and add salt and/or pepper if required.

Second layer filling: Peel and chop the eggs, finely chop the dill. (Do not mix with the trout mousse.)

LAYERING THE SANDWICH CAKE:

Layer 1 – On a flat serving plate, place three pieces of bread side-by-side, butter up, and cover with half of the tuna mix. Cover with another three pieces of bread, butter up, criss-crossing the first layer.

Layer 2 – Spread the smoked trout mousse over the bread, cover with the chopped hard-boiled eggs and dill. Place three pieces of bread on top, butter up, side-by-side as in layer 1.

Layer 3 – Cover the third and final filling layer with the remaining tuna mix, then place the last three unbuttered slices of bread on top, criss-crossing as in layer 2.

> **NOTE: You will get the best and tastiest result, if you make the cake up to this point one day ahead, cover with plastic cling wrap and refrigerate.**

Garnish: Mix the mayonnaise and crème fraîche then spread the cake top and sides with the mixture. Garnish the sides with lettuce leaves.

Topping/decorating: Decorate the sandwich cake just before serving, using your own imagination for the best presentation – however you decorate it, this seafood sandwich cake is sure to impress even the most discerning of your guests!

Ham and paté sandwich cake
Smörgåstårta med skinka och leverpastej

SERVES 16–18

20 slices white bread,
cut lengthwise

FIRST AND THIRD LAYER

200g/7 oz smoked ham,
thinly sliced

200ml (³/₄ cup plus 1 tbsp)
crème fraîche

150ml (¹/₂ cup plus 1 tbsp)
mayonnaise

2 tbsp mustard

20g (¹/₂ cup) parsley, finely
chopped

SECOND LAYER FILLING

200g/7 oz chicken liver pâté

75ml (¹/₂ cup plus 3 tsp) cream

150g/5.3 oz pickled cucumber,
thinly sliced

GARNISH

200ml (³/₄ cup plus 1 tbsp)
mayonnaise

200ml (³/₄ cup plus 1 tbsp)
crème fraîche

TOPPING/DECORATIONS

200g/7 oz smoked ham,
thinly sliced

200g/7 oz sliced cheese,
e.g. Jarlsberg or Masdaam

1 cucumber

100g/3.5 oz black grapes

Radishes

Cocktail tomatoes

Maiche or other soft-leaf lettuce

Prepare the bread: Remove the crusts from all slices and butter 15 slices, leaving 5 unbuttered. Buttering the bread helps to 'stabilise' the cake and counteracts the potential for the bread to go 'mushy'.

First layer filling: Cut the ham into small cubes and mix with the crème fraîche, mayonnaise, mustard and parsley – taste and add salt and pepper if required.

Second layer filling: Mix the paté and cream to a smooth and spreadable paste, and cut the pickled cucumber into thin slices.

LAYERING THE SANDWICH:

Layer 1 - On a big flat serving dish place two slices lengthwise and then butt up with three slices vertically to create a rectangle, with all slices butter side up. Spread half of the ham filling on the base then cover with another round of bread, butter side up – this time starting with three slices vertically butted up by two slices horizontally. Criss-crossing the bread this way makes the cake stay together better.

Layer 2 - Spread all of the paté filling on the second layer and top with the pickled cucumber slices. Cover with bread slices, butter side up, layered the same way as the base.

Layer 3 - Spread the remaining ham filling and cover with the remaining unbuttered bread.

> NOTE: You will get the best and tastiest result if you make the cake up to this point one day ahead, cover with plastic cling wrap and refrigerate.

Garnish: Mix the mayonnaise and crème fraîche and spread on the top and sides of the cake.

Topping/decorating: Decorate the sandwich cake just before serving. Thinly slice the cucumber and press onto the sides of the cake. Using your own creativity, decorate the sandwich cake with the ham, cheese, grapes, cocktail tomatoes, sliced or quartered radishes and lettuce.

Three small gourmet sandwiches
Tre små lyxsmörgåsar

This entrée dish follows the theme of the landgång but by serving as individual sandwiches allows greater flexibility and also uses fewer ingredients. The principle of serving a combination of fish/seafood, meat and cheese remains unchanged however — they sure do make a colourful and mouth-watering presentation. And they never disappoint!

Use bread of your choice — white, multigrain, rye, or sourdough. Remove the crust and use the bread square, or cut to form round or triangle shapes.

FISH/SEAFOOD SANDWICH – TOPPING SUGGESTIONS

Prawns, hard-boiled eggs, mayonnaise
GARNISH: lettuce, sliced cucumber, tomato, lemon and dill

Pickled herring, sliced cold potatoes, hard-boiled eggs, sour cream
GARNISH: red/Spanish onion rings, dill and chives

Smoked salmon/gravlax and gravlax sauce
GARNISH: lettuce, capers, hard-boiled egg slices, red/Spanish onion rings, lemon, dill

MEAT SANDWICH – TOPPING SUGGESTIONS

Rare roast beef and horseradish cream
GARNISH: lettuce, fried shallots, pickled cucumber, tomato, sliced orange, parsley

Meatballs and beetroot salad
GARNISH: lettuce, sliced cucumber, red pepper/capsicum, tomato, sliced orange, parsley

Ham and horseradish cream
GARNISH: lettuce, sliced cucumber, red pepper/capsicum, tomato, sliced orange, parsley

CHEESE SANDWICH – TOPPING SUGGESTIONS

Slices of hard cheese such as Jarlsberg, Maasdam or Emmenthaler
GARNISH: lettuce, sliced cucumber, red and green pepper/capsicum, tomato, sliced radishes, chives

Brie and/or camembert with prunes or fresh figs
GARNISH: lettuce, sliced cucumber, tomato, black grapes

Blue cheese with pears and walnuts
GARNISH: lettuce, red pepper/capsicum, parsley

"Old Man's Mix"
Gubbröra

This delicious egg and anchovy mix goes by the colourful name Gubbröra, which translates to 'Old man's mix'. It is served either as a stand-alone dish on the Swedish smörgåsbord, or as an appetiser served on top of cold sliced potatoes on rye or crisp bread and garnished with dill and chives.

SERVES 4–6

4 hardboiled eggs

100g/3.5 oz Swedish anchovies, pickled dill or matjes herring

2 tbsp red/Spanish onion, finely chopped

2 tbsp chives, finely chopped

2 tbsp dill, finely chopped

2 tbsp crème fraîche

3 tbsp egg mayonnaise

Chop the anchovies (or pickled dill or matjes herring) and eggs into small cubes, and mix with the finely chopped red onions, chives and dill. Mix the crème fraîche and mayonnaise together and add to the herring and egg mix.

Serve as a stand-alone dish on your smörgåsbord or as an appetiser by topping rye or crisp bread with the mix and garnishing with dill, chives, lemon slices and perhaps for some extra colour cocktail tomatoes.

For a more substantial appetiser, you can also add some cold sliced potatoes as a base on the crisp or rye bread.

MAINS —
FISH & SEAFOOD

Salmon, potato and dill bake
Laxpudding

Laxpudding is another classic dish — especially on the smörgåsbord — and another of my favourite dishes. Apart from the basic ingredients of salmon and potatoes, it's the creamy milk and egg mix along with the dill that appeals so much to my taste buds. Traditionally, it is served with melted butter poured all over it! Very rich indeed. However, these days as we all have become more health conscious the melted butter is replaced by lemon wedges.

SERVES 4–6

2 tbsp butter

500ml (2 cups) full cream milk

100ml (¹/₃ cup plus 1 tbsp) thick cream

4 large eggs

1 tsp sea salt flakes

¹/₂ tsp ground white pepper

1kg/2.2 lb potatoes, peeled and thinly sliced

1 brown onion, finely chopped

400g/14 oz fresh salmon, skin off, sliced thinly or 300g/10.5 oz smoked or cold-cured salmon

25g (¹/₂ cup) dill, finely chopped

Preheat the oven to 200°C/400°F.

Grease a high-sided, round ovenproof dish. Whisk the milk, cream, eggs, salt and white pepper together in a large bowl. Layer potatoes (first and last layers), onions, salmon, and dill, and pour over the egg mix. Probe around the edges and centre to ensure the mix evenly covers the potato and salmon layers.

Bake in the oven for about one hour – or longer if the egg mix has not settled (loosely cover with foil if the top starts to turn too brown). Remove from the oven and brush with melted butter for extra shine. Leave to settle for about 10 minutes before serving.

To serve the traditional way, plate the salmon pudding then pour melted butter over each portion. Or, for a healthier version, forget the melted butter and just serve with lemon wedges.

Gravlax with gravlax sauce

Gravlax med gravlax sås

The word gravlax is now known the world over as one of the most renowned Swedish dishes – salmon fermented in a salt, sugar and dill mixture for up to two days. Sounds like a lot of work, but of course nothing could be further from the truth – it only takes around ten minutes to prepare, and then all you have to do is turn it now and then as it matures.

Traditionally served with new season or dill creamed potatoes, it is always accompanied by lemon wedges and a sweet mustard and dill sauce. Gravlax is both delicious and nutritious and can be eaten all year round.

These days as the majority of salmon is farmed, there is a prevailing view that the salmon should be frozen for at least 48 hours before preparing to eliminate any potential parasites. If not frozen before preparing, the gravlax can be frozen for up to 3 months.

SERVES 6–8

1kg/2 lb 3 oz side of fresh salmon, centre cut, skin on

25g (¼ cup) finely crushed sea salt

110g (½ cup) sugar

25g (½ cup) dill and stalks, coarsely chopped

20 coarsely crushed white peppercorns

Clean and fillet the salmon and remove any bones with tweezers. Wipe the salmon dry with paper towels and cut in half. With a small sharp knife pierce the skin at the thickest part of the fish. Mix the salt, sugar, pepper and dill and spread approximately ¼ of the cure mixture on the bottom of a snap-lock plastic bag. Place one fillet on the spice mixture, skin down. Spread approximately half of the remaining mixture over the fillet. Place the second fillet on top, skin up and head part over the tail part. Sprinkle over the remaining cure mixture.

Place the plastic bag in a glass or porcelain dish and leave to sit at room temperature for 2 hours to allow the sugar and salt mix to start melting. Weigh the salmon down by putting a small chopping board or platter on top. This will push any moisture out of the fish and speed up the curing process. Put in the fridge to mature for 48 hours, turning the salmon over a few times when the juices start to collect. Don't be concerned about the amount of liquid that leaks out, just pour it away daily then turn the salmon and re-position the weight.

To serve, scrape off any residue spice mix and pat dry with paper towels. Slice thinly using a very sharp knife, keeping it at an acute angle, starting at the thin end of the salmon.

When ready to serve, remove most of the spice mix, garnish with fresh dill and lemon wedges. Serve with toast, new season or dill-creamed potatoes, and gravlax sauce. The gravlax will keep in the fridge for up to a week. It also freezes really well, and will keep for up to 3 months.

VARIATIONS:

❀ Add a shot of your favourite clear spirit, e.g. gin, vodka or aquavit, and pour over the meat side of the fillet right before putting it in the fridge.

❀ Add 2–3 raw, peeled and coarsely grated beetroot (about 250g/9 oz) and 4 tbsp grated horseradish (fresh or from a jar) to the cure mixture then proceed as per recipe above. You will end up with a deep red salmon, with a slightly earthy flavour. This version is best served with a different kind of sauce, for example the caviar and red onion sauce on page 46.

Gravlax sauce

Gravlaxsås

3 tbsp sweet mustard

¼ tsp ground mustard seeds

2 tbsp sugar

2 tbsp red wine vinegar

100ml (⅓ cup plus 1 tbsp) canola oil

Dill, finely chopped to taste

Salt and pepper to taste

1 tbsp brandy (optional)

Combine the mustard, ground mustard seeds, sugar and vinegar and whisk until the sugar is completely dissolved. Slowly add the oil while whisking vigorously. Add the dill then set aside to infuse for 30 minutes. Taste and add salt and pepper, and more dill and/or ground mustard if required. Lastly add the brandy if using. Chill before serving.

Hot-pickled salmon

Inkokt lax

Another very traditional way to cook salmon, especially in summer, is to hot pickle it, then serve cold with (the ever present) new season potatoes, dill and lemon – and of course a sauce, this time of the sour cream and mayonnaise variety. Add some greens, either lettuce, spinach or even green beans, and you have a light and nutritious meal, equally delicious for lunch or dinner.

SERVES 4–6

1 kg/2 lb 3 oz fresh salmon

2 tsp salt

1 bay leaf

6 white peppercorns

8 dill sprigs

½ brown onion, sliced

1 carrot, sliced

500ml (2 cups) warm water

50-100ml (¼ – ½ cup) white vinegar

Clean and rinse the salmon, removing any small bones with tweezers and cut into 3–4cm/1 inch thick portions. In a low, wide saucepan, add the spices, dill, onion and carrot slices, vinegar and water and bring to the boil. Cover with a lid and simmer for approximately 10 minutes. Taste the stock and add more spices or vinegar if desired. Add the salmon and gently simmer for 8–10 minutes. Move the salmon and stock to a serving dish and let it cool.

Serve with new season potatoes and mayonnaise sauce.

Mayonnaise sauce

Majonnässås

200ml (³/₄ cup plus 1 tbsp) good quality egg mayonnaise

200ml (³/₄ cup plus 1 tbsp) sour cream or crème fraîche

Salt and white pepper to taste

Mix the mayonnaise and sour cream and season with salt and pepper. You can also spruce up the mayonnaise sauce by adding any of the following:

❀ 25g (¹/₂ cup) chopped dill, chives, tarragon or parsley – or any combination thereof

❀ 80g (¹/₂ cup) chopped pickled vegetables

❀ 50ml (¹/₄ cup) chilli sauce or tomato ketchup with a few drops of lemon juice

Cold-cured salmon

Rimmad lax

This dish is my personal favourite when it comes to the plethora of ways to prepare and enjoy salmon. Although when done, the salmon resembles that of gravlax, it is in fact quite different in taste and texture. It is simply irresistible served with creamed potatoes or zucchini, and as much as this combination sounds very rich and heavy, it is surprisingly refreshing and light.

The perfect balance between sweet and salty is crucial to get the desired final result, which is why the salt is measured by weight rather than volume — salt granules can vary enormously insize and thus distort the true amount of salt used.

These days as the majority of salmon is farmed there is a prevailing view that the salmon should be frozen for at least 48 hours before preparing to eliminate any potential parasites. If not frozen before preparing, the pickled salmon can be frozen for up to 3 months.

SERVES 4-6

STAGE 1 - CURING

1kg/2.2 lb fresh salmon, skin on, bone free, middle piece

75g/2.6 oz sea salt flakes

55g (¹/₄ cup) sugar

STAGE 2 – BRINE IMMERSION

100g/3.5 oz sea salt flakes

1L (4 cups) cold water

Stage 1 - Put the salmon in a glass or porcelain dish, meat side up. Mix the sea salt and sugar and rub into the fish. Leave to sit at room temperature for about 2 hours to start the curing process. Turn the salmon over, i.e. meat side down, loosely cover with cling wrap and keep in the fridge for 24 hours. There is no need to turn the salmon during this process.

Stage 2 – Mix the sea salt and cold water in a dish big enough to hold the salmon - remove the salmon from the curing dish and put it the brine. Cover with cling wrap and put in the fridge for another 15 hours.

When done, slice the salmon very thinly (best done using a fish carving knife with a flexible, long blade) and serve with creamed new season potatoes (see the Side Dishes section), a green salad and lemon wedges.

Ovenbaked salmon
with feta and pink pepper
Ugnsbakad lax med feta ost och rosé peppar

This tasty and festive dish is really quick to make and the combination of feta, pink pepper and cream accompanies the salmon beautifully. You can use portion sized salmon as in the recipe, or if you prefer to use a whole side of salmon, simply adjust the quantities of ingredients. This dish, where the cream mixture covering keeps the salmon moist and pink, is equally lovely served for lunch as for dinner.

SERVES 4

4 salmon portions, skin off

¼ organic stock cube (or more to taste)

300ml (1 ¼ cups) thick cream

100ml (⅓ cup plus 1 tbsp) dry white wine

Zest from ½ lemon

1 tsp tomato paste

15g (¼ cup) fresh chopped dill

1 tsp salt

1 tsp white pepper, ground

150g/5.3 oz feta, crumbled

2–4 tbsp whole pink peppercorns

Preheat the oven to 200°C/400°F.

Put the salmon portions in an ovenproof dish. Dissolve the stock cube in a little hot water. Combine the cream, wine, lemon zest, tomato paste, dill, salt and pepper and add the stock cube liquid. Spread the mix evenly over the fish. Scatter the crumbled feta and pink peppercorns over the salmon portions.

Bake in the oven for 15 to 20 minutes, depending on how well cooked you want the salmon to be. If you have a thermometer, the inner temperature of the salmon should not be less than 55°C/140°F.

Serve with new season potatoes, green string beans and asparagus spears.

Fried sardines with dill and parsley filling
Stekt strömming med potatismos

Strömming is also called Baltic herring, and is smaller than the Atlantic herring found in the North Sea. It is more like a sardine and is sold as such in most countries outside Scandinavia. It's found in abundance in the brackish waters of the Baltic Sea, making strömming a very affordable staple of the Swedish diet. These days however it has been elevated to a more gourmet status and is regularly served as Today's Special in many cafes and lunch restaurants.

SERVES 4–6

30 sardines, cleaned, gutted, skin on

3 eggs

400ml (1 ½ cups plus 1 tbsp) milk

3 tbsp Dijon mustard

3 tbsp sweet mustard

Salt and pepper

60g (½ cup) plain flour

60g (½ cup) breadcrumbs

15g (¼ cup) fresh dill and parsley, finely chopped

Rinse the sardines in cold water and cut off the back fins, keeping the sardines intact. Place in a sieve to drain off any excess water.

Whisk the eggs, milk and mustard together and add a good pinch of salt and pepper. Put the sardines in the marinade and leave for 1-2 hours, ensuring all sardines are fully immersed.

Mix the flour and breadcrumbs. Remove the sardines one by one from the egg mixture. Put one sardine skin side down, add some finely chopped parsley and dill and put another sardine on top, skin up. Turn the butterfly sardines in the flour and crumb mix then fry in butter over moderate to high heat for approximately 2–3 minutes on each side.

Serve with mashed potatoes, lingonberries and vegetables of your choice.

NOTE: Leftover sardines make a great lunch served on crisp bread with cold sliced potatoes (or even leftover mash), and garnished with red onion rings and more dill.

Lemon marinated salmon with caviar and red onion sauce

Citronmarinerad grillad lax med kaviar- och rödlökssås

Barbecuing has become something of an obsession in Sweden over the past decade or so, and one of the most popular ways to eat salmon in summer is to marinade it then cook it on the barbecue. This recipe is just one of literally hundreds, and proves how the Swedish love affair with fish, dill, cream and potatoes has adapted beautifully to this method of cooking.

SERVES 8–10

1.3kg/2 lb 14 oz fresh salmon, skin on

100ml (¹⁄₃ cup plus 1 tbsp) olive oil

Zest and juice of 1 lemon

1 tbsp honey

25g (¹⁄₂ cup) finely chopped dill

1 tsp sea salt flakes

1 tsp white ground pepper

Mix the olive oil, lemon juice and zest, honey, dill, sea salt and pepper to make a marinade. Put the salmon in a dish, skin side down, and pour over the marinade. Place the salmon in the fridge for approximately 2 hours, turning 3–4 times. Remove the salmon from the dish and cook on the barbecue, skin side down, for 10–15 minutes. Don't be concerned if the skin gets burnt, just remove it before serving.

Using a serving plate, or a saucepan lid, turn the salmon meat side down and slide onto the grill. Barbecue the salmon for another 3–5 minutes.

Serve with a fresh green salad, new season potatoes and a caviar and red onion sauce.

Caviar and red onion sauce

Kaviar och rödlök sås

150ml (¹⁄₂ cup plus 1 tbsp) crème fraîche

150ml (¹⁄₂ cup plus 1 tbsp) mayonnaise

1 small red/Spanish onion, finely chopped

2 tbsp red caviar

25g (¹⁄₂ cup) dill, finely chopped

2 tbsp lemon juice

Salt and pepper

Mix the crème fraîche with the mayonnaise, onion, caviar, dill and lemon juice. Add salt and pepper to taste.

Meatballs with cream sauce
Köttbullar med gräddsås

SERVES 4-6

1 brown onion

3 tbsp breadcrumbs

1 egg

4 tbsp cream

2 tsp salt

1 tsp white pepper

300g/10.5 oz ground beef

200g/7 oz pork mince

CREAM SAUCE

100ml (⅓ cup plus 1 tbsp) beer

1 tbsp mustard

200ml (¾ cup plus 1 tbsp) cream

Chop the onion finely and fry until soft without gaining colour, set aside to cool. Combine the onion with the cream, breadcrumbs, salt, pepper and the egg, add the ground beef abd pork and combine into a smooth mixture. Cover and refrigerate for 30 minutes.

Fry one sample meatball, taste and adjust seasoning as required. For smaller sized meatballs, roll level tablespoons of the mixture into balls, and a heaped tablespoon for medium sized balls.

For nice round meatballs, use your hands to roll the meatballs and keep wetting them as you go. Cook the meatballs for about 6–10 minutes (depending on size) over medium heat in batches, shaking the pan regularly to brown all over. Continue until all the meatballs are cooked, but do not wash the pan between batches.

Move the cooked meatballs onto a serving dish and keep warm. Add the beer to the pan juices, scrape the bottom to loosen any meat that remains then simmer until half the liquid has evaporated. Combine the pan juices with the mustard and cream and simmer for 5 minutes – taste and add more mustard, salt or pepper if required.

Serve with mashed potatoes, the cream gravy (served separately) fresh pickled cucumber and lingon berry preserve. If lingon berries are not available thencranberry conserve is a good substitute.

Beef Rydberg
Biff Rydberg

This classic Swedish dish, Biff Rydberg, is said to originate from the once opulent Hotel Rydberg in Stockholm, where it was first served. Hotel Rydberg was a favourite haunt for artists, authors and musicians, but sadly was demolished in 1914 to make room for a new, modern bank building!

Biff Rydberg is the upmarket version of the more common pyttipanna (bubble and squeak). The basic ingredients of potatoes, onion and meat are the same, but Beef Rydberg doesn't use smoked meat and the beef is always premium fillet steak. It is also plated individually.

The pyttipanna on the other hand traditionally relies on leftover roast meat and potatoes, with some smoked sausage or bacon thrown into the mix and served from the pan.

SERVES 4

8 large potatoes

600g/1 lb 5 oz beef fillet

2 large brown onions

50g/1.8 oz butter

4 egg yolks

15g (¼ cup) parsley, finely chopped

MUSTARD CREAM

100ml (⅓ cup plus 1 tbsp) crème fraîche

1 tbsp Dijon mustard

1 tsp ground yellow mustard seeds

To make the mustard cream, mix the crème fraîche with the Dijon mustard and ground mustard seeds, set aside in the fridge for 30 minutes to allow the flavours to develop.

Peel and cube the potatoes to approx 15mm in size. Rinse under running water to remove the starch. Cut the beef fillet into 15mm cubes, and chop the onion coarsely.

Fry the onions over medium heat in the butter until soft and translucent, remove from pan. Fry the potatoes until golden, but take care not to overcook them, they need to retain some of their crunchiness. You can also parboil the potatoes for 5 minutes, drain and steam dry before frying.

Just before serving, fry the beef in a very hot pan and season with salt and pepper.

Arrange the potatoes, onion and beef on individual plates, and serve with an egg yolk and the mustard cream. If a raw egg yolk is not your thing, you can add a fried or poached egg instead.

Traditional condiments are chopped pickled beetroot, dill cucumber, and chives – these can also be arranged on each plate.

Beef fillet in pastry

Inbakad oxfilé

This dish is one that my sister loved to cook back in the 1970s and still does today. It is a great main course for a dinner party as it can be prepared well in advance and assembled and cooked on the day. It is particularly appreciated by the male guests; perhaps it is because it can be likened to a fancy version of the humble meat pie!?

SERVES 4

500g/1 lb beef fillet, in one piece

1 brown onion

50g/1.8 oz mushrooms

1 tbsp butter

2 egg yolks

100g/3.5 oz chicken liver pâté

1 sheet of puff pastry

Preheat the oven to 200°C/400°F.

Season the beef fillet with salt and pepper and fry until brown all around, approximately 3–4 minutes on each side. Set aside to cool.

Chop the onion and mushrooms, but not too finely. Sautee in butter over medium heat until all the liquid has evaporated, Remove from the heat and add one egg yolk, season with salt and pepper and spread out on a plate to cool.

Spread a layer of the chicken pâté on the pastry and top with half of the cold mushroom mix. Place the cold beef fillet on top, and then spread the remainder of the mushroom mix on top of the fillet. Roll the pastry over the fillet, making sure it is completely covered. Brush with beaten egg yolk. Bake in the middle of the oven for 30 minutes.

Allow to rest for a few minutes before carving. Serve with your favourite salad or steamed vegetables and potato wedges.

> **NOTE:** It's important that the meat is properly seared before it's baked in the pastry – this allows the flavour to deve op and avoids meat juices leaking. Also, make sure the meat and the mushroom mix are cold when assembling, to prevent the pastry going soft while baking.

Barbecued pork fillet
Helgrillad fläskfilé

Pork is the most favoured meat in the Swedish cuisine – and comes in many guises. Pork fillet along with the pork 'scotch fillet steak' are the preferred meat for the barbecue. The versatility of the pork fillet in particular is reflected in the hundreds of recipes you will find in cook books, online recipe sites, blogs, and in recipes passed on from one generation to the next. Here are just three of many marinades adding flavour and punch to the mild pork fillet meat.

To keep the pork fillet juicy and moist when barbecuing whole, keep the temperature medium and grill for no longer than 15-20 minutes depending on the thickness of the fillet. Here are a couple of marinades to try; each will need a minimum of 2 hours to do their work effectively.

SERVES 4

MARINADE 1

100ml (¹/₃ cup plus 1 tbsp) red wine

1 tbsp balsamic vinegar

2 tbsp olive oil

100ml (¹/₃ cup plus 1 tbsp) crème fraîche

50ml (¹/₄ cup) chilli sauce

1 tsp salt

1 tsp white pepper

¹/₄ organic vegetable stock cube

MARINADE 2

Juice and rind of 1-2 lemons

1-2 crushed garlic cloves

100ml (¹/₃ cup plus 1 tbsp) olive oil

3 tbsp chopped parsley

1 tsp salt

1 tsp white pepper

MARINADE 3

Zest of 1 lemon

120ml (¹/₂ cup) freshly squeezed lemon juice

120ml (¹/₂ cup) virgin olive oil

2 tbsp green peppercorns

1 tbsp chopped fresh rosemary

1 tbsp chopped fresh thyme

1 tsp salt

Clean the pork fillet by removing any fat and sinew. Mix the ingredients for the marinade and pour over the fillet, either in a plastic sealable bag or in a bowl, ensuring it is completely covered. Leave to marinate in the fridge for at least 2 hours, preferably longer – overnight even.

The best method to barbecue a whole pork fillet is by the indirect method, or on the lowest heat if using a gas barbecue. Use a meat thermometer positioned in the thickest part of the fillet and cook for about seven minutes on each side – or until the inner temperature is 67°C/152°F (it will continue to rise to about 70°C/158°F when removed from the heat).

If you do not have a meat thermometer, after seven minutes on each side, turn again and cook for another couple of minutes each side.

Remove from the barbecue, cover and rest for approx 15 minutes before cutting into 20mm thick slices. Serve with a fresh salad, asparagus and steamed greens.

Beef patties with onion pan juices

Pannbiff med lök

This dish in all its simplicity is one often served in Swedish lunch restaurants, as its few ingredients and no-nonsense approach makes it not just easy to make, but ensures it never disappoints. There's something childishly satisfying about mashing your pristine boiled potatoes into the onion jus and create your own version of mashed potato!

SERVES 4

1 large egg

100ml (⅓ cup plus 1 tbsp) full cream milk

3 tbsp breadcrumbs

Salt and white pepper

500g/1 lb ground beef

3 large brown onions

Combine the egg and milk then add the breadcrumbs and stand aside to rest for 10 minutes. Add a good pinch of salt, pepper and the ground beef and work to a smooth mix. Shape into patties, place on a lined baking tray, cover and put in the fridge for 30 minutes.

Slice the onions and cook over medium heat until soft, golden and almost caramelised. Transfer the onions to a side dish and keep warm. Fry the patties over medium heat until brown on both sides and cooked through then remove to a heated serving platter. Put the onions back into the pan, add approximately 100ml (⅓ cup plus 1 tbsp) of water and/or stock, heat and season to taste.

Serve the patties with the onion jus, boiled or fried potatoes, lingon berries, pickled cucumber and crisp snow peas.

Beef a la Lindström

Biff a la Lindström

The Beef a la Lindström at first glance could be seen as a red version of the standard beef patty. However, the inclusion of chopped beetroot and capers makes these patties something very different — they're earthy, moist, salty, sweet and crunchy all at the same time.

They're most commonly served with a potato and cream gratin, but in our family we eat 'Lindströmmarna' with creamed cabbage, boiled potatoes and fermented cucumber . . . sounds an odd combination but let me assure you, it works!

SERVES 4

1 large egg

100ml (⅓ cup plus 1 tbsp) full cream milk

3 tbsp breadcrumbs

Salt and white pepper

2 tbsp onion, finely chopped

500g/1 lb ground beef

3 tbsp pickled cucumber, finely chopped

2 small pickled beetroots, finely chopped

2 tbsp small capers

Mix the egg, milk and breadcrumbs. Set aside to rest for 10 minutes. Add a good pinch of salt and pepper. Chop the onion finely and fry for about 2 minutes or until soft and translucent. Let cool, then add to the bread crumb mix, along with the meat. Cover with cling wrap and put in the fridge for 30 minutes.

Add the cucumber, beetroot and capers to the meat mix and shape into patties. Fry over medium heat for 3–4 minutes each side.

Scatter capers and chopped pickled cucumbers over the patties and serve with potato gratin and beetroot, or creamed cabbage, boiled potatoes and beetroot.

Swedish bubble & squeak

Pyttipanna

Pyttipanna is one of those versatile dishes that turn leftovers into a sure dinner winner. Traditionally, leftovers from the Sunday roast would be used but these days it is made with any combination of meat leftovers — steak, chicken, roast, ham, bacon and even meatballs. Add some day old boiled potatoes and onion and top with a fried egg and presto, there you have a very tasty and satisfying meal.

SERVES 4-6

8-10 boiled potatoes, cold

500g/1 lb cubed meat (beef, smoked bacon, ham or sausage)

2 brown onions

4 tbsp parsley, finely chopped

4-6 eggs

Preheat the oven to 200°C/400°F.

Cut the potatoes and meat into cubes about 1.5cm/½ inch in size. Chop the onions finely.

Fry the potatoes until golden then put into a large ovenproof dish. Sautee the onions until soft and golden, add to the potatoes. Next fry the meat, if fresh cook on medium-high heat and if using leftovers on medium heat.

Mix the meat with potato and onion, add salt and pepper, and keep warm in the oven while poaching or frying the eggs.

Sprinkle the parsley over the pyttipanna and serve with eggs, beetroot, mustard, pickled cucumber, Worcestershire sauce and a green crisp salad.

Pork chops in creamy mustard sauce

Fläskkotletter med gräddsås

The most often served meat when I grew up in Sweden was pork — and whenever I visit the homeland I find pork is still as popular as ever. It is not expensive and the meat is soft and mellow in taste. The pork chop is as versatile as chicken, as it can be matched with virtually any spice, herb or condiment — from the very mild to the very hot. My family is particularly fond of this version — mild enough for the young yet tasty enough for the older folks.

SERVES 4

4 pork chops, with the bone

Salt and pepper

250ml (1 cup) dry white wine

3 tbsp wholegrain mustard, unsweetened

¼ vegetable stock cube

300ml (1¼ cups) thick cream

Parsley and chives, chopped

Put a sheet of baking paper over the chops and press down with the palm of your hand to flatten the meat. Fry each side of the pork chop in butter for about 1 minute over medium-high heat, then for another 2 minutes over medium heat. Add salt and pepper to taste then remove the chops from the pan and keep warm.

Add the wine to the pan juices and simmer for a couple of minutes. Add the mustard, stock cube and cream and simmer for another couple of minutes. Taste and add more mustard, salt or pepper as required. Sprinkle chopped parsley and chives over the sauce.

Serve with green beans, carrots and potatoes, pasta or rice.

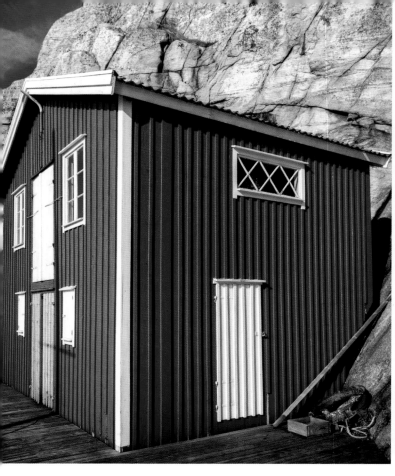

SIDE DISHES

Creamed dill potatoes
Dillstuvad potatis

Creamed potatoes with dill — this is a real classic that speaks to all lovers of potatoes. This dish is best using freshly boiled potatoes, but can also be made using cold, leftover potatoes. Creamed dill potatoes is the first choice of side dish to go with smoked or cold-cured salmon, but works equally well served alongside grilled sausages or pork chops.

SERVES 4–6

12–14 medium-sized potatoes

2 tbsp butter

3 tbsp plain flour

400ml (1 ½ cups plus 1 tbsp) whole milk

100ml (⅓ cup plus 1 tbsp) cream

Salt and white pepper

25g (½ cup) dill, finely chopped

Peel the potatoes, put in lightly salted water and boil until just soft. Drain and set aside to cool, then slice or cube the potatoes.

Melt the butter in a saucepan large enough to hold the potatoes. Sift the flour over the melted butter and stir until smooth, then slowly add the milk while stirring. Bring to just under the boil, and while stirring gently, add the cream and simmer for a couple of minutes. Add salt and pepper to taste, followed by the dill.

Gently fold in the potatoes and simmer until the potatoes are heated through.

Creamed cabbage
Stuvad vitkål

Creamed cabbage is a highly undervalued and seldom cooked dish — and yet due to its gentle flavour when creamed, it can be served with almost any meat; grilled sausage or chicken, meatballs, beef patties or even with fried tofu or haloumi. It's not the most impressive looking side dish, but once you've tried it, you're sure to cook it more than once.

SERVES 4

500g/1 lb cabbage

500ml (2 cups) water

$1/2$ tsp salt

2 tbsp butter

3 tbsp plain flour

400ml ($1^1/_2$ cups plus 1 tbsp) milk

2 tbsp parsley, finely chopped

Pinch of ground nutmeg

Salt and pepper

Prepare the cabbage by removing the outer leaves, and any parts with marks or blemishes. Quarter the cabbage and remove the core. Shred the quarters and put into boiling salted water – bring back to the boil and cook for 5 minutes, test for desired softness and continue cooking for another couple of minutes if required. Drain the cabbage in a sieve.

Melt the butter in a saucepan large enough to hold the cabbage. Sift the flour over the melted butter and whisk until smooth, then slowly add the milk, a little at a time, while stirring. Bring to just under the boil and simmer for 5 minutes, then add the cooked cabbage and heat through. Add salt and pepper to taste, followed by the chopped parsley and ground nutmeg.

> **TIP: Carrots, peas, cauliflower and beans are also aptly suited for 'creaming', just follow the recipe above and substitute the cabbage for the vegetable of your choice . . . equally delicious, especially the creamed beans!**

Potato gratin
Potatisgratäng

This particular potato gratin is usually served alongside oven-baked whole eye fillet — it's the garlic and leek that combine to superbly match the fillet. The gratin is also soft and creamy, not just because it uses a healthy amount of cream, but because the potatoes are first boiled in cream and milk, rather than water. This is comfort food at its elegant best.

SERVES 4–6

1kg/2 lb firm potatoes

$1/2$ leek, white part only

2 garlic cloves

400ml ($1^1/_2$ cups plus 1 tbsp) cream

400ml ($1^1/_2$ cups plus 1 tbsp) milk

4 tbsp breadcrumbs

25g/1 oz soft butter

Salt and pepper

Preheat the oven to 180°C/350°F.

Peel the potatoes and slice thinly, preferably in a food processor for even thickness. Rinse and finely slice the leek then peel and crush the garlic cloves.

Fry the leek and garlic in butter in a big saucepan until soft, fragrant and translucent. Add the cream and milk and bring to the boil. Add the sliced potatoes, salt and pepper to taste. Bring back to the boil and simmer until the starch has dissolved and the mix is thick and creamy. Keep stirring to ensure the mix doesn't burn at the bottom of the pan.

Pour the potato and cream mixture into an ovenproof dish, sprinkle with breadcrumbs and a few dobs of butter. Cook for 30 minutes. Check for firmness of the potatoes and cook for another 5–10 minutes if required.

Potato gratin with cheese

Potatisgratäng med ostlager

SERVES 4–6

12 medium-sized potatoes

1 brown onion

3 tbsp butter

170g (1²/₃ cups) grated tasty cheese

1¹/₂ tsp salt

1 tsp ground white pepper

400ml (1¹/₂ cups plus 1 tbsp) cream

4 tbsp breadcrumbs

Pre-heat the oven to 225°C/400°F.

Peel the potatoes and put into a dish with cold water to avoid discolouring. Chop the onion and fry in 1 tbsp of the butter until soft and translucent, approximately 5 minutes. Slice the potato, preferably in a food processor for even thickness.

In a greased ovenproof dish, put one layer of potato on the bottom, sprinkle over some grated cheese, onion, salt and pepper. Repeat until all potatoes, cheese and onion have been used.

Pour over the cream and add some dollops of butter. Cook for 35–40 minutes then remove from the oven and add the breadcrumbs. Cook for another 10–15 minutes.

Potato wedges

Klyftpotatis

Potato wedges are beautiful served as a snack with sour cream and sweet chilli sauce, or accompanying grilled meat, hamburgers or roasts. The key to make them soft on the inside and crunchy on the outside is to pre-boil the potatoes, then bake in a hot oven. You can also add almost any spice to the finished product — garlic salt, lemon pepper, paprika — the choice is only limited by your own imagination.

SERVES 4–6

1kg/2 lb firm potatoes

¹/₂ tsp salt

4 tbsp olive or canola oil

2 tbsp dried thyme

2 tbsp sea salt

Pre-heat the oven to 250°C/500°F.

Scrub the potatoes clean and cut each into 6–8 wedges. In a saucepan add ample amount of water to cover the wedges and ¹/₂ tsp salt. Bring to the boil and add the potato wedges – simmer for 3 minutes. Remove the potatoes, put in a colander to drain and steam dry.

Mix oil, thyme and salt in a large bowl, add the potato wedges and mix to coat. Put the wedges on an oven tray lined with baking paper and bake in the oven for about 15 minutes, turning a couple of times.

Mashed potatoes
Potatismos

Is there any other food that screams comfort as much as a soft and creamy serving of mashed potatoes? Well, perhaps it has a few competitors, still, mashed potatoes go with just about anything and I have not yet met anyone who does not like it. For a more upmarket presentation, add an egg and put the mash in the oven until golden and crusty.

SERVES 4-6

1kg/2 lb potatoes

200ml (³/₄ cup plus 1 tbsp) whole milk

25g/1 oz butter

Salt and pepper to taste

Pinch of ground nutmeg

Peel the potatoes, cut into smaller pieces and place in a saucepan. Bring to the boil in lightly salted water, reduce the heat and simmer for 10–15 minutes or until soft, then drain. Heat the milk and butter in another saucepan and pour over the potatoes.

Mash with a fork or potato masher then whisk, preferably with an electric beater until light and fluffy. Try not to whisk for more than a couple of minutes, otherwise the mash may get sticky from the high release of starch. Add salt, pepper and nutmeg to taste – or more butter to make the mash really rich and creamy.

Creamed zucchini with dill and lemon
Dillstuvad zucchini

The creamed zucchini with dill and lemon is a surprisingly delicious companion to cold-cured salmon (see page 43). When I was first served this dish, I thought 'ohh, this may be just far too rich for me', and therein lay the surprise — it's simply not. The cured salmon is light and not fatty, and the mellow flavour of the zucchini suits it perfectly — and of course the lemon and dill add to the taste experience as well.

SERVES 4

600g/1.3 lb zucchini/courgette

3 tbsp butter

1 tsp salt

Grated zest of 1 lemon

3 tbsp flour

300ml (1¹/₄ cups) light cream

50g (1 cup) dill, finely chopped

Peel and cut the zucchini into 1cm pieces – or leave the skin on if you prefer. Heat the butter in a saucepan and fry the zucchini for about one minute. Add salt and lemon zest.

Add the flour and gently mix with the zucchini pieces. Add the cream and stir, then simmer for approximately two minutes. If you leave the skin on, the zucchini may need cooking for another minute. Mix in the dill just before serving.

SOUP

Seafood soup with saffron and herbs
Fisksoppa med saffran och örter

It is the fennel, saffron and herbs that make this seafood soup stand out in a crowd — it is a good thing when nutritional value meets with beautiful taste. It is my absolute favourite seafood soup, and I often served it as a dinner party starter — it's tasty, not too heavy, and really wakes up those taste buds for the dishes that follow ... Or serve it as a main course with crusty bread and perhaps a hard cheese — it's equally popular either way.

SERVES 4

400g/13 oz fresh or frozen cod or other firm white fish such as saithe or haddock

300g/10 oz fresh or frozen skinless salmon

150g/5 oz cooked and peeled prawns

1 leek

1 fennel bulb

2 carrots

250ml (1 cup) water

2 fish or vegetable stock cubes

250ml (1 cup) dry white wine

10-15 strands of saffron (0.5g approximately)

1 tsp dried thyme

1 tsp dried basil

1 tsp salt

½ tsp ground white pepper

250ml (1 cup) reduced cream

100ml (⅓ cup plus 1 tbsp) crème fraîche

If using frozen fish or prawns, plan ahead and thaw in the fridge so they retain their flavour, firmness and freshness.

Thoroughly clean the leek, remove the outer parts then cut the white part into thin rings. Remove the outer layer of the fennel and cut into thin strips. Peel the carrots and cut into 1cm cubes or half moons.

Gently fry the leek, fennel and carrot in a little oil on medium-high heat for 3-4 minutes.

In a big stainless steel saucepan, heat the water and immerse the stock cubes, stir to mix. Add the fried vegetables and the white wine, saffron, salt, pepper, dried thyme and basil and simmer for 10 minutes.

Cut the cod and salmon into 3cm/1 inch cubes and add to the soup along with the cream and crème fraîche. Bring to the boil and simmer gently for 5-6 minutes or until the fish is cooked through. Taste the soup and adjust the seasoning as required. Just before serving add the prawns, reserving a few to use as a garnish.

Ladle the soup into bowls, garnish with some prawns and serve with sourdough bread – great for soaking up the liquid at the bottom of the bowl!

TIP: To intensify the colour and flavour of the saffron, infuse it in a little hot water before adding it to the soup.

Mushroom and celeriac soup
Svampsoppa med rotselleri

A creamy, tasty and nutritious soup made with mushrooms and celeriac. Serve with crispy bacon, rye or crisp bread and a nutty hard cheese. Mushrooms are another food that is perfect for everyone — packed with fibre, antioxidants and vitamins. Mushrooms are also so distinct in nature they are classified as their own category, fungi, as their composition is separate from that of vegetables. They are a great source of B vitamins and minerals, are low in calories, fat free and contain very low levels of salt.

This recipe combines the health benefits of mushrooms with those of the root celery (celeriac), which is rich in vitamin K and many essential minerals, such as phosphorus, iron and calcium.

SERVES 4

4 bacon rashes, finely diced

1 small brown onion

200g/7 oz celeriac (root celery)

250g/9 oz button mushrooms

1L (4 cups) vegetable stock

200ml (³/₄ cup plus 1 tbsp) reduced cream

Salt and pepper

20g (¹/₂ cup) parsley, finely chopped

Remove the fat from the bacon rashes, then finely dice and fry until crisp. Set aside.

Peel the onion and celeriac and wipe the mushrooms clean with paper towels, keeping stems intact. Coarsely chop the onion, celeriac and mushrooms.

In a large stainless steel saucepan gently fry the mushroom, celeriac and onion for 5 minutes. Pour in the vegetable stock, cover and simmer for about 10 minutes or until the celeriac is soft. Add the cream and bring to the boil.

Add the parsley to the soup and process using a hand mixer until it is silky smooth. Ladle into serving bowls and garnish with the bacon pieces and a little parsley. Serve with crusty or crisp bread and a hard, nutty cheese.

Spring vegetable soup
Vårprimörsoppa

This spring vegetable soup is a classic that is usually served at Easter, when spring in the Northern Hemisphere brings the first tender vegetables of the season. It is sweet, tender and light as well as bright and colourful.

SERVES 4

4 chicken thigh fillets, on the bone

1L (4 cups) water

1 small cauliflower

6 new season carrots, small

3–4 tbsp plain flour

250ml (1 cup) full-cream milk

10 asparagus spears

130g (1 cup) fresh peas

150g/5 oz snow peas

50g/2 oz spring onions/scallions

50g/2 oz baby spinach

200ml (³/₄ cup plus 1 tbsp) thick cream

50g/2 oz chopped chives

Trim the chicken thighs by removing the skin and most of the fat. Cook the chicken in a saucepan of lightly salted water for about 10 minutes, or until they are cooked through. Remove from the broth and remove the chicken meat from the bones, but do not discard the liquid. Set the chicken meat aside.

Rinse the cauliflower and break into bouquets. Peel the carrots and cut into discs. Cook the cauliflower and carrot discs in the chicken broth for about 8 minutes. Remove the vegetables and put the chicken broth through a fine-mesh sieve to remove any small solids.

Pour the strained broth back into the saucepan, whisk together the flour and milk and pour into the broth. Bring to the boil, reduce the heat and simmer for 2 minutes. Rinse and trim the asparagus and spring onions and cut into bite-size pieces, but keep some of the green part of the spring onion for garnish.

Add the asparagus, peas, spring onions, baby spinach, cauliflower and carrots to the soup and bring to the boil. Add salt and pepper to taste.

Whip the cream until semi-soft and fold into the soup just before serving. Garnish with the chicken meat and chives.

Green pea soup
Grön ärtsoppa

This brilliantly green soup is made from fresh or frozen green peas. It is quick to make and its gentle flavor will appeal to the whole family as a weekday dinner. It can also be easily made more luxurious by adding some dry champagne and served as an entrée at a stylish dinner party. The champagne is added right at the end to the finished soup and garnished with mint leaves.

SERVES 4

1 brown onion

1L (4 cups) water

1 vegetable stock cube

6 sprigs of parsley

200ml (³/₄ cup plus 1 tbsp) dry white wine

600g/1.3 lb frozen green peas

100ml (¹/₃ cup plus 1 tbsp) crème fraîche

Fresh mint leaves

Chop the onion finely and cook in a little butter or oil until soft and translucent. In a stainless steel saucepan, bring the water and stock cube to the boil and add the onions along with the parsley sprigs and wine. Bring back to the boil and simmer for 10 minutes.

Pour the stock liquid through a sieve and discard the onions and parsley. Pour the stock back into the saucepan, add the peas, bring back to the boil and simmer for 5 minutes.

With a hand mixer, process the peas until the soup is silky smooth. Whisk in the crème fraîche and add salt and pepper to taste. Garnish with mint leaves.

Spinach soup with mushroom and bacon
Spenatsoppa med bacon och champinjoner

SERVES 4

400g/13 oz fresh baby spinach

200g/7 oz mushrooms

6 bacon rashes, fat removed

60g/2 oz butter

5 tbsp plain flour

1L (4 cups) full cream milk

500ml (2 cups) vegetable stock

Salt and white pepper

Rinse the spinach leaves to remove any grit or impurities. Wipe the mushrooms using a paper towel and cut in half, then slice – if the mushrooms are very big cut in half then half again before slicing. Cut the bacon rashes into strips, fry until crisp and set aside. Keep some bacon strips for garnish.

Melt the butter over medium-low heat in a large stainless steel saucepan. Add the flour and stir until smooth and bubbling, about 1–2 minutes. Remove from the heat and slowly add the milk one cup at a time, whisking continuously until very smooth. Return to the heat, add the stock, salt and pepper and cook for 5 minutes, stirring constantly.

Add the bacon pieces, mushroom slices and spinach to the soup and bring to the boil, then simmer for 5 minutes.

Ladle into bowls and garnish with crispy bacon pieces and chives.

Fish soup with prawns, dill and tomato

Fisksoppa med räkor, dill och tomat

This is another beautiful fish soup that is not only addictively moreish, but will also satisfy the most ravenous of the family due to the inclusion of both potatoes and vegetables. The fish the Swedes use for their fish soups is cod, but any firm white fish will work equally well if cod is not available. Also, with the addition of prawns and baguette croutons it is sufficiently festive to serve as an entrée at a dinner party.

SERVES 4

400g/13 oz fresh or frozen cod or other firm white fish such as saithe or haddock

8 small potatoes

1 brown onion

1 carrot

800-900ml (3¼–3½ cups) fish or vegetable stock

2 tomatoes

200ml (¾ cup plus 1 tbsp) crème fraîche

Salt and pepper

Juice of 1 small lemon

25g (½ cup) roughly chopped dill

200g/7 oz peeled prawns

1 sourdough baguette

Olive oil

You can use any firm white fish but a nice piece of fresh or frozen cod is the preferred option. If using frozen fish and/or prawns, prepare by allowing sufficient time to thaw in the fridge to retain flavour, firmness and freshness.

Cut the fish into 3cm/1 inch cubes. Peel the potatoes, onion and carrot. Cut the potatoes and onion into 3cm/1 inch cubes, and carrot into slices or half moons (depending on the size of the carrot). In a large stainless steel saucepan, gently fry the vegetables in a little butter for 4 minutes, then add the stock. Bring to the boil then reduce the heat and simmer for 10 minutes.

Submerge the tomatoes in hot water then remove the skins and roughly chop. Add the crème fraîche and the tomatoes to the vegetables and bring to the boil. Add salt and pepper to taste, followed by the lemon juice.

Add the fish to the soup and simmer for 4 minutes. Add most of the chopped dill and simmer for another minute or two – check that the fish is cooked through. Just before serving add the prawns, keeping some aside for garnish. Ladle into soup bowls, add a few prawns and garnish with the remaining dill on top.

Serve the soup with sourdough baguette croutons – simply slice the baguette, brush with olive oil and bake in the oven at 250°C/500°F for about 8 minutes.

Salmon and spinach soup

Lax och spenatsoppa

This is a soup that is easy on the eye and packed full of vitamins, antioxidants and omega-3, and pulls a punch in the flavour department to boot. The addition of sourdough croutons adds crunch and are delicious when used to soak up the tasty broth.

SERVES 4

600g/1.3 lb fresh salmon fillet, skin off

1 yellow capsicum/pepper

1 red capsicum/pepper

1 brown onion

1L (4 cups) water

1 fish or vegetable stock cube

100ml (⅓ cup plus 1 tbsp) crème fraîche

250g/9 oz chopped spinach

Salt and white pepper

1 sourdough baguette

Olive oil

Clean the salmon then remove any pin bones and rinse in cold water. Cut into 5cm/2 inch cubes and set aside.

Clean the capsicums then remove the core and cut into 1cm/½ inch squares. Peel and cut the onion into thin wedges. In a stainless steel saucepan, cook the capsicum and onion in a little butter until soft and the onion is translucent.

Add the water and stock cube to the vegetables and bring to the boil then reduce the heat to a simmer. Gently fold the crème fraîche into the soup, followed by the spinach. Add salt and pepper to taste.

Add the salmon pieces to the soup and simmer gently for 5 minutes.

Meanwhile slice the baguette and brush the slices with olive oil. Bake in the oven at 250°C/500°F for about 5 minutes. Cut the slices into quarters and add to the soup, or serve separately.

Carrot, cauliflower and parsnip soup
Blomkålssoppa med morot och palsternacka

Not the most pretty of dishes, but this is a great vegetarian soup that blends the mellow flavour of cauliflower with the sweetness of carrot and the earthiness of parsnip. It is also typical of the kind of food eaten in Sweden for centuries, where the locals relied on seasonal vegetables, specifically root vegetables, which thrive in the cold Scandinavian climate. For the non-vegetarians in the family, topping the soup with crisp bacon or other smoked meat is a savoury option.

SERVES 4

1 small cauliflower

2 carrots

2 small potatoes

1 parsnip

1 leek

1L (4 cups) water

1 vegetable stock cube

100ml (¹/₃ cup plus 1 tbsp) reduced cream (optional)

100ml (¹/₂ cup) chopped parsley

Salt and pepper

Clean the vegetables and peel the root vegetables. Break up the cauliflower into small bouquets – keep a few aside for garnish at the end. Cut the carrots, potatoes and parsnip into 3cm/1 inch cubes. Slice the leek, white and light green parts only.

Bring the water to the boil in a saucepan and add the stock cube. Put the carrots, potatoes and parsnip into the stock and simmer for 8 minutes or until just soft. Add the cauliflower and leek and continue simmering for another 5 minutes until all vegetables are soft. Add salt and pepper to taste.

Process the soup with a hand mixer until silky soft – taste the soup and add more salt or pepper if required.

Add the cream if using and stir until mixed through – or serve the cream on the side. Sprinkle with chopped parsley and serve with rye bread and a hard cheese.

DESSERT

DESSERT — OR COFFEE AND CAKE?

When it comes to desserts, Swedes are generally not as enamoured with this concept as many other cuisines. They tend to be keener on cakes, buns and biscuits as they more naturally fit with that most Swedish of traditions – Fika. In other words, sit down together for a coffee, catch up on what's going in life and chomp away at one of the many delicious cakes on offer. It is even more common to do this at home with family and friends than it is going out for a coffee. Whenever you visit someone at their home, a 'fika' is the first offer of refreshment you will receive.

There is even a degree of incredulity and consternation if you are not up to yet another 'fika' on the day . . . Not surprising when you consider that the Swedes consume more coffee per capita than any other country in the world. The coffee is brewed and often drunk black, rather than the Italian versions – espresso, latte, cappuccino and the like. This is probably one of the main reasons why the espresso machine has not made strides into Swedish homes the way it has in other Western countries.

So, it is proper then to include some desserts here that work equally well as a 'fika' accompaniment, just delete the ice cream or vanilla custard. The berry or fruit-based desserts are also often served as a mid-morning or afternoon snack, or even breakfast. For breakfast the soup or compote would be served with crunched crisp bread and milk for a filling and nutritious start to the day.

Apple cake with vanilla custard is one of the most loved dessert in Sweden, so it is only fitting that here I offer three options – and leave it up to you to pick the one that most appeals to your palate. Having said that, they are all without doubt seriously delicious.

The kladdkaka, aka Swedish Sticky Chocolate Cake (!), is a serious competitor for the No 1 dessert-cum-cake . . . it is gooey, chocolatey, sticky and is accompanied with lots of whipped cream. The choice is all yours!

Apple cake with cinnamon-marinated apples

Äppelkaka med kanelmarinerade äpplen

This recipe is a little unusual in that it 'marinates' the apple slices in a sugar, cinnamon and vanilla sugar mix. The longer the apples are infused, the more pungent the apple and spice mix will permeate through the cake. You can even let the apples infuse in the spice mix for up to eight hours. Prepare in the morning and presto, ready to use when baking the apple cake in the evening!

It's a sure bet this cake will become a favourite amongst family and friends — or perhaps you will make it for your own (guilty?) pleasure again, and again, and again . . .

SERVES 8–10

3 tbsp caster sugar

1 tbsp cinnamon

½ tbsp vanilla sugar

3 large apples

150g/5 oz butter, at room temperature

220g (1 cup) caster sugar

3 eggs

190g (1½ cups) plain flour

1 tsp baking powder

50ml (¼ cup) full cream milk

Pre-heat the oven to 175°C/350°F.

Grease a round springform cake tin, approximately 24cm/9 inch in diameter. Dust lightly with plain flour.

In a bowl combine the sugar, cinnamon and vanilla sugar. Peel, core and halve the apples, then cut into 1cm/½ inch cubes. Add the apple cubes to the cinnamon mix and toss to cover all over, set aside. The best result will be achieved if the apples are left to 'marinate' in the sugar and cinnamon mix for at least a couple of hours, but preferably longer.

In a bowl, mix the room temperature butter and sugar and beat with a hand mixer until the sugar is dissolved and the mix is light and fluffy. Add one egg, stir until the mixture is smooth then add the other eggs, repeating the process. In a separate bowl combine the flour and baking powder then gently stir the flour into the cake batter until smooth. Lastly, slowly stir in the milk and mix.

Pour the cake mix into the baking dish then evenly spread the apple cubes on top and push them into the cake. Lastly drizzle the 'marinade' liquid that the apples were sitting in over the cake.

Bake in the middle of the oven for 40 minutes, check if the cake is ready by inserting a skewer, if still wet bake for another 5 minutes.

Remove from the oven and let stand for a couple of minutes before releasing the sides of the tin and moving the cake to a serving dish. Serve lukewarm with vanilla custard, ice cream or a dollop of cream.

If serving the apple cake cold, add a dusting of icing sugar, or mix icing sugar with water and drizzle over the cake.

Apple cake with cinnamon and cardamom

Äppelkaka med kanel och kardemumma

This is a very moist, sweet and tasty apple cake; it's delicious as a cake on its own or served as a dessert along with vanilla custard or ice cream. It is quick and easy to make, where the soft and moist cake meet crunchy cinnamon and sugar covered apple slices. Add to this the sweet cardamom and almond sprinkled top and you have a fabulously moreish cake where one piece simply will not do! It is best served soon after baking and while still warm, but will keep well for another couple of days (if it lasts that long).

SERVES 8-10

200g/7 oz butter, at room temperature

220g (1 cup) caster sugar

2 tsp vanilla sugar

3 eggs

230g (1³/₄ cups plus 1 tbsp) plain flour

2 tsp baking powder

75ml (¹/₃ cup) full cream milk

4 apples

2 tbsp cinnamon

2 tbsp caster sugar

2 tsp ground cardamom

2 tbsp caster sugar

3 tbsp almond meal

Pre-heat the oven to 175°C/350°F.

Grease a round springform cake tin, approximately 24cm/9 inch in diameter. Dust lightly with flour.

Cut the room-temperature butter into cubes and add to a bowl with the sugar and vanilla sugar. With a hand beater, or in a mixer, beat the butter and sugars together until white and fluffy. Add one egg, stir to thoroughly combine then add the second egg and continue stirring before adding the final egg.

In a separate bowl, mix the flour and baking powder. Gently fold the flour into the cake batter and stir until smooth, then add the milk and stir gently to combine. Pour the batter into the prepared spring-form cake tin.

Rinse and core the apples, leaving the skin intact. Mix the cinnamon and sugar together. Cut the apples in half then into thin wedges, place in a bowl and sprinkle over the cinnamon and sugar mix and toss to coat. Note that the apple wedges will be unevenly covered by the cinnamon mix.

Push the apple wedges into the cake mix all the way to the bottom, lengthwise with skin facing up – they should be a tight fit.

Mix the cardamom, sugar and almond meal and sprinkle over the top.

Bake in the lower part of the oven for 30 minutes. Check with a skewer and if still moist, bake for another 5 minutes. Let stand for a couple of minutes to settle before unclasping the springs. Serve lukewarm with vanilla custard, ice cream or cream.

Or, if serving as part of a 'fika' session, it will delight just as it is alongside a cup of brewed coffee.

Upside down caramelised apple cake
Upp-och-nervänd äppelkaka

This recipe is very versatile in that here we are using apples, but you can also use pears, peaches or plums, and even thin slices of pineapple. It is also quick and easy to make from ingredients usually found in the cupboard — just add some fruit. It could be a favourite of those who perhaps are not too keen on cinnamon, as it breaks away from the traditional apple-cinnamon combination.

SERVES 8-10

155g (1¼ cups) plain flour

330g (1½ cups) caster sugar

1 tsp baking powder

100g/3 oz butter

1 egg

50g/2 oz butter

2 tbsp light brown sugar

1½ tsp cinnamon

25g (¼ cup) flaked almonds (optional)

4 apples

Pre-heat the oven to 175°C/350°F.

Mix the flour, sugar and baking powder in a bowl. Gently melt the butter and set it aside to cool. Add the egg to the batter and stir gently to combine. Pour the melted butter into the mix and combine.

Grease a baking dish (not a springform tin) and dust lightly with flour. Combine the butter, brown sugar and cinnamon in a small saucepan over low heat – when melted add the almond flakes, if using, and boil very quickly, for 30 seconds only. Scrape the butter and sugar mix into the baking dish and spread evenly over the bottom.

Peel and core the apples, cut in half and slice thinly into half-moon shaped discs. Cover the bottom of the dish with the apple slices, pressing down to level.

Pour the cake mix over the apples and bake for 30 minutes. Check the cake by inserting a skewer and if still wet, bake for another 5 minutes. Remove from the oven and leave the cake to cool for a couple of minutes before turning it on to a serving platter, with the caramelised apples facing up.

Serve the cake lukewarm with vanilla custard, ice cream or a dollop of cream flavoured with 1 tsp of vanilla sugar.

Blueberry soup – or compote
Blåbärssoppa eller blåbärskräm

Other than popping freshly picked, sweet and juicy blueberries into your mouth there is no better way to savour this nutritious and colourful berry than in a homemade blueberry soup or compote. It is easy to make, can be eaten as soup, drunk as a detoxing juice, or by adding a bit more potato flour will turn it into a blueberry compote. So there really is no reason not to try this recipe at home, especially as either fresh or frozen blueberries can be used. The good news is that blueberries have one of the highest antioxidant capacities of all fruits and vegetables. Recent studies also show that frozen blueberries are equally as high in antioxidants as fresh blueberries. This is reassuring if you do not have ready access to fresh blueberries — and means year-round availability of delicious and nutritious blueberries.

The bilberry, related to the blueberry, is a native to Northern Europe and grows in the wild, as it does in North America, and has been used for centuries both medicinally and as a food. In Sweden, it even grows close to urban areas as long as forested land is left intact. The bilberry is smaller, flatter and more acidic than the sweet, round blueberry, but carries even more antioxidants and vitamins. If by chance you are using bilberries, you may need to add a bit more sugar to the recipe.

SERVES 8

1 liter fresh or frozen blueberries

1L (4 cups) water

110g (½ cup) sugar

1–3 tbsp potato flour

If you are fortunate enough to have access to freshly picked blueberries, clean and rinse the berries to remove any dirt or impurities. If using store bought fresh berries, rinse to remove any residue or dust.

Put the water and sugar in a big stainless steel saucepan, bring to the boil and stir until the sugar is completely dissolved. Add the blueberries, stir and cook for no more than 3 minutes then remove from the heat.

Do a taste test and if required add a little more sugar. In a small bowl, mix the potato flour and enough water to make a runny paste. Add the potato paste tablespoon by tablespoon until the desired thickness is reached then put the soup back on the heat and bring to the boil – remove from the heat as soon as bubbles start to appear.

Serve the blueberry soup either warm or cold – Swedes prefer the soup served cold with a dollop of whipped cream if served as a dessert.

It can also be served for breakfast or as a snack – crunched crisp bread is often added for a filling and nutritious mid-morning or afternoon snack.

Blueberry crumble
Smulpaj med blåbär

This is a beautiful dessert — it's got colour, it's got elegance, it's got flavour. And it's full of vitamin and antioxidant rich blueberries. Swedes prefer this version of a berry pie, i.e. without a pastry base — just a sweet pastry crumble sprinkled on top.

You can use either fresh or frozen berries but as frozen berries generate liquid when thawed, you need to stabilise the berries by adding a little potato flour.

SERVES 4

470g (2 ³/₄ cups plus 1 tbsp) fresh or frozen blueberries

1 tbsp potato flour, if using frozen berries

55g (¹/₄ cup) caster sugar

PASTRY CRUMBLE

125g (1 cup) plain flour

50g (¹/₂ cup) oats

4 tbsp sugar

Pinch of salt

150g/5 oz butter

Pre-heat the oven to 200°C/400°F.

First make the pastry crumble – add the flour, oats, sugar and salt to a bowl and mix. Rub the butter into the flour mix with your fingertips until the mixture resembles breadcrumbs. Leave to rest for 20 minutes.

Grease an ovenproof pie dish. If using fresh blueberries, arrange the berries at the bottom of the dish and sprinkle with sugar.

If using frozen berries, thaw the berries in a sieve to drain the juice. Mix the blueberry juice with 1 tbsp of potato flour then mix with the blueberries. Arrange the berries at bottom of the pie dish and sprinkle with sugar.

Crumble the pastry evenly over the blueberries.

Bake the pie in the middle of the oven until the crumble is golden, about 20-30 minutes. Remove the pie from the oven and leave to cool before serving.

Serve the blueberry pie lukewarm with custard or ice cream.

Oven baked semolina pudding with cordial sauce

Mannagrynspudding med saftsås

This dessert requires a bit of commitment by the home cook — it has several steps from the initial semolina porridge base to the making of cordial sauce. Let me assure you though, it is worth the extra effort and is a dessert blessed with the life-long love of many children! The silky smooth oven-baked semolina pudding rates very high on the scale of comfort foods, and the cordial sauce adds to that comfort experience. Plus it adds a festive and colourful look to what otherwise could be a somewhat bland presentation. Of course the cordial sauce can be substituted for a raspberry coulis made from fresh berries, but it would no longer be a true traditional experience!

By the way, semolina porridge is often served for breakfast with a dob of butter, sprinkled with cinnamon and a little sugar and ice-cold milk poured onto the side of the bowl so as not to interfere with the melting butter!

SERVES 4–6

SEMOLINA PORRIDGE

1L (4 cups) full cream milk

100g (½ cup plus 1 tbsp) semolina

½ tsp salt

SEMOLINA PUDDING

Pre-made semolina porridge

2 tbsp sugar

Zest of 1 lemon

75g (½ cup) raisins

2 eggs

CORDIAL SAUCE

100ml (⅓ cup plus 1 tbsp) black currant or raspberry cordial

400ml (1½ cups plus 1 tbsp) water

1 tbsp potato flour

Pre-heat the oven to 200°C/400°F.

Grease an ovenproof dish of about 1.5L (6 cups) capacity.

SEMOLINA PORRIDGE

In a large saucepan bring the milk and salt to the boil. Whisk in the semolina and reduce the heat. Simmer for 5 minutes stirring regularly to prevent the milk and semolina burning or sticking to the side of the pan. Remove from the heat and let cool before embarking on the next step, the semolina pudding.

SEMOLINA PUDDING

Combine the lukewarm or cold semolina porridge with sugar, lemon zest and raisins. Add the eggs one at a time and gently fold into the porridge. Pour the semolina porridge into the oven proof dish and bake for 20–25 minutes, or until the pudding is golden brown.

CORDIAL SAUCE

Mix the potato flour and a little water to make a runny paste.
In a stainless steel saucepan combine the water, cordial and potato flour mix. Whisk constantly while bringing to the boil then gently simmer for 1 minute.

Pour the sauce into a jug when sufficiently cooled. Sprinkle sugar on top to avoid a surface skin forming.

Serve the semolina pudding warm or cold, with the cordial sauce.

Rice à la Malta

Ris à la Malta

Ris à la Malta is traditionally eaten at Christmas in Scandinavia, but of course can be eaten all year round. The name Ris à la Malta is believed to be a distortion of the Danish dish Risalamande, the first version of this dessert in Scandinavia, and which in turn stems from the French dish Riz à l'amande. In other words, the name of the dish has absolutely nothing to do with its namesake the island of Malta, but everything to do with France and almonds.

The Danish version Risalamande was created in the early 1900s. It is believed that when rice porridge became an everyday dish for the Danish population, the upper classes wanted to refine it by adding expensive ingredients such as cream, almonds and vanilla and for it to be served as a dessert.

Whatever its name, this is a very satisfying and a little decadent dessert, loved by the young and old alike. It is a little laborious to make but definitely worth the effort.

SERVES 4–6

RICE PORRIDGE

170g (³/₄ cup plus 1 tbsp) pearl rice

400ml (1¹/₂ cups plus 1 tbsp) water

¹/₂ tsp salt

1 tbsp butter

1 cinnamon stick

750ml (3 cups) full cream milk

¹/₂ tsp vanilla sugar

4 tbsp almond flakes, optional

RIS À LA MALTA

2 oranges

1 mandarin

150ml (¹/₂ cup plus 1 tbsp) thick cream

1 tsp vanilla sugar

RICE PORRIDGE

Rinse the rice under running cold water. Put the rice and water in a large stainless steel saucepan. Add the salt, butter and cinnamon stick. Bring to the boil over medium heat then cover and simmer for about 10 minutes.

Pour in the milk and stir gently. Bring the porridge back to the boil, cover and simmer very gently for about 40 minutes without stirring. Add the vanilla sugar and almond flakes and stir gently to mix – set aside to cool then refrigerate until completely chilled.

RIS À LA MALTA

Peel the oranges and cut into smaller pieces. Gently fold the orange pieces into the cold rice porridge. Peel the mandarin and divide into wedges to be used as a garnish.

Whip the cream until firm then fold in the vanilla sugar and mix. Fold the whipped cream into the chilled pudding.

Divide the Ris à la Malta into serving bowls and garnish with the mandarin wedges. You can also sprinkle a little cinnamon over the dish before garnishing with the mandarin wedges.

Rhubarb compote
with cinnamon cream
Rabarberkräm med kanelgrädde

Rhubarb thrives in the colder Northern Hemisphere climate and features heavily in the Swedish cuisine during summer. Rhubarb is in fact a perennial herb displaying attractive and succulent deep red leafy stalks. Being a herb, it is low in calories, full of vitamins, dietary fibre and antioxidants such as B-complex vitamins and vitamins A and K.

Rhubarb is used in drinks, in pies and of course in the form of compote. The taste is not as sweet as summer fruits and berries (apart from the gooseberry) and it is the sweet-tart flavour of the rhubarb that is so palatable. Combined with cinnamon, vanilla, a little sugar and served with cream, this is as simple and satisfying as a dessert can be.

SERVES 4

600g/1.3 lb red rhubarb (about 10 stalks)

400ml (1 1/2 cups plus 1 tbsp) water

165g (3/4 cup) caster sugar

1 cinnamon stick

2 tbsp potato flour

4 tbsp water

TO SERVE

1 tsp ground cinnamon

2 tsp icing sugar

300ml (1 1/4 cups) whipping cream

Rinse the rhubarb and cut into 1.5cm/1/2 inch pieces. Bring the water, sugar and the cinnamon stick to the boil in a stainless steel saucepan. Add the rhubarb pieces and gently cook for about 3 minutes or until the rhubarb starts to break down. Remove the pan from the heat.

Mix the potato flour and water to make a smooth runny paste. Slowly pour the paste into the rhubarb compote, gently stir to incorporate then put the saucepan back on the heat. Bring to the boil, gently stirring, and as soon as bubbles appear remove from the heat. Remove the cinnamon stick.

Mix the ground cinnamon and icing sugar and stir into the cream that has been whipped to desired consistency. Serve the rhubarb warm or cold with the cinnamon cream.

TIP: For a smoother compote, peel the stalks and cook for 5 minutes or until all the rhubarb pieces have broken up – this version may appeal more to children.

PICKLED &
FERMENTED
FOODS

A FEW PICKLING TIPS

Pickling and fermenting food is an ingenious way to preserve seasonal produce – fish, vegetables, fruit and even meat. The formula for the pickling liquid tends to vary from vegetable to vegetable, from fruit to fruit, as well as personal taste. The Swedish palate steers towards a sweeter taste, whereas the Germans, for example, prefer the vinegar to be the prominent flavour.

The basic formula we use for pickling is the 1-2-3 method:

1 part vinegar (double strength 11–12%)

2 parts sugar

3 parts water

This is then adjusted to the produce being pickled – to individual taste and to sugar content of the produce. Where the recipe calls for double strength vinegar – approx 12% acidity – this is noted, otherwise use normal strength of around 5% acidity.

It is also important to properly sterilise pickling jars and equipment – this will keep the pickles in good condition for the prescribed period. To prepare glass preserving jars, ensure there are no chips or cracks, first wash in hot, soapy water then thoroughly rinse. Boil the jars and lids in a large saucepan for a minimum of 15 minutes.

If the recipe calls for the hot pickling liquid to be poured over the produce, ensure the jar is warm as it may crack otherwise.

Pickled strawberries

Inlagda jordgubbar

Strawberries are definitely the berry of choice during the wonderful but brief Nordic summer. They have a special place in the hearts of Swedes as they are always at their best around Midsummer, and are a must at the Midsummer celebrations. However, this recipe goes against the trend of eating the strawberries fresh, yet is a lovely way to spruce them up with mint and spices. These pickled strawberries are delicious served on top of ice cream or plain yoghurt, or on a cheese board.

1kg/2 lbs fresh strawberries

1 sprig of fresh mint

6 white peppercorns

1 cinnamon stick

2 whole cloves

4 whole cardamom pods, cracked

190ml (³/₄ cup) apple cider vinegar, normal strength

190ml (³/₄ cup) water

110g (¹/₂ cup) sugar

Clean and rinse the strawberries, cut off the tops and drain the fruit on a piece of paper towel. Halve or quarter the strawberries depending on size and place in a sterilised glass jar, layering the mint, strawberries and spices.

Mix the vinegar, water and sugar in a stainless steel saucepan and bring to the boil while stirring until the sugar is dissolved. Allow to cool slightly then pour over the strawberries. Cool to room temperature before putting in the refrigerator for a minimum of 12 hours before serving. The strawberries will keep for up to three weeks in the refrigerator.

Pickled lemons

Inlagda citroner

This recipe diverts from the more common preserved lemon method of applying salt to cut lemons then steeping in either water or lemon juice. Instead it uses the Nordic pickling method, resulting in a sweeter and more complex flavour by the addition of cinnamon and cloves.

1kg/2 lbs lemons

1 cinnamon stick

3 whole cloves

500ml (2 cups) water

25g (¹/₄ cup) sea salt

250ml (1 cup) apple cider vinegar

¹/₂ tsp whole white pepper

1 bay leaf

110g (¹/₂ cup) caster sugar

Clean the lemons thoroughly to remove any impurities, pat dry. Quarter or slice the lemons and put them into a large sterilised glass jar with a tight-fitting lid. Add the cinnamon stick and cloves and place so they're clearly visible for presentation purposes.

Combine the water, salt, vinegar, pepper, bay leaf and sugar in a stainless steel saucepan and bring to the boil then reduce the heat and simmer for a couple of minutes. Cover the lemons with the hot pickling liquid and tightly close the lid.

Set aside in your pantry for 4 weeks before consuming. Once the jar is opened, keep the pickled lemons refrigerated.

Pickled vegetables

Inlagda grönsaker

These colourful pickles are a tasty, versatile and nutritious condiment to barbecued meat, chicken or even salmon, and add colour and crunch alongside a classic cheese omelette. Use your favourite vegetables in season and mix and match for colour and personal taste! The ability of pickled vegetables to improve gut flora has long been known to contribute to overall health and wellbeing.

1kg/2 lbs mixed vegetables of your choice, e.g. carrots, cauliflower, squash, broccoli, zucchini/courgette, green beans, green tomatoes, brown or red/Spanish onion, mini corn, eggplant/aubergine and red and yellow capsicum/pepper.

STEP 1 – BRINE LIQUID

50g (½ cup) sea salt flakes

1L (4 cups) water

STEP 2 – PICKLING LIQUID

500ml (2 cups) water

2 bay leaves

200ml (¾ cup plus 1 tbsp) white or apple cider vinegar, double strength

1-2 cinnamon sticks

385g (1¾ cups) caster sugar

½ tsp whole white pepper

1 tbsp whole allspice

4 whole cloves

Step 1 – Mix the salt and water in a bowl large enough to hold the vegetables. Rinse, clean and peel the vegetables as required and cut into equally sized pieces. If using 'hard' vegetables, blanch for a few minutes then drop into ice cold water to stop the cooking. Add the vegetables to the brine and leave in the fridge for 8–10 hours.

Step 2 – Mix all ingredients for the pickling liquid and bring to the boil then reduce the heat and simmer gently for a couple of minutes. Drain the brine liquid from the vegetables and put them into sterilised glass jars. Pour over the hot pickling liquid (leave about 2cm/1 inch of headroom) and tightly close the lids. Let cool before putting in the fridge. Have a trial taste after about 2 weeks; the pickled vegetables will keep in the fridge for at least a couple of months.

Pressed Cucumber

Pressgurka

This delicate fermented-pickled cucumber is the perfect companion to robust meat dishes, such as steak and roast, and is a must with meatballs, mash and cream gravy. The combination of short fermentation with salt, followed by cold pickling adds extra flavour and crunch, making this one of the all-time favourite pickles in Swedish homes. It can also be consumed in as little as a couple of hours after preparing, making it ideal for the time-poor cook.

1 cucumber, sliced very thinly

1 tsp salt

2 tbsp apple cider vinegar, double strength

100ml (⅓ cup plus 1 tbsp) water

4 tbsp sugar

¼ tsp ground white pepper

2 tbsp parsley, finely chopped

Clean the cucumber then slice as thinly as possible – shaved even – and combine with the salt in a wide bowl. Place a plate on top and weigh it down with a heavy dish or can. Let the mixture stand on the kitchen counter for about 30 minutes then gently squeeze the cucumber slices to drain away the liquid that has formed. Combine the vinegar, water, sugar, pepper and parsley and stir until the sugar has completely dissolved. Put the cucumber slices in a jar or serving dish and cover with the pickling liquid. Leave for at least 2 hours before serving.

Fermented cucumber

Inlagd saltgurka

This particular fermented cucumber is called 'salt-cucumber' in Swedish due to the process of first fermenting it in salty brine before the traditional pickling stage. This gives a sweet-sour flavour to the finished pickle — and makes the cucumbers longer lasting than the speedier method of pickling alone. The most common way to eat the salt-cucumber is on crisp bread topped with chicken liver paté.

1kg/2 lbs small cucumbers, each approximately 10cm/4 inches long

STEP 1 - BRINE LIQUID

1L (4 cups) water

50g (½ cup) sea salt flakes

STEP 2 - PICKLING LIQUID

500ml (2 cups) water

200ml (¾ cup plus 1 tbsp) apple cider vinegar, double strength

440g (2 cups) sugar

2 tsp whole white peppercorns

2 tbsp yellow mustard seeds

Dill and dill crowns – add more dill sprigs if you cannot find dill crowns

Step 1 – Clean the cucumbers to remove any impurities. Mix the water and salt for the brine and add the cucumber. Leave to ferment for at least 8 hours.

Step 2 - Remove the cucumbers from the brine and drain on a clean towel. Mix the ingredients for the pickling liquid in a stainless steel saucepan and bring to the boil. Reduce the heat and allow to simmer gently for a few minutes. Layer the cucumber, dill and dill crowns in a large sterilised glass jar with a tight-fitting lid and cover completely with the hot pickling liquid. Seal the lid tightly and leave the jar to cool on the bench before transferring it to the refrigerator.

The cucumber will be ready to eat in about 1 week, and will keep for up to 3 months in the fridge.

20-minute pickled cucumber

Snabbinlagd gurka

Sometimes all you want is a savoury condiment that is quick, easy and nutritional. Well, this recipe will provide that – it's ready in around 20 minutes. Add it to your grilled meat, roast chicken, meatballs, or put it on an open sandwich with cheese, pâté or cold cut meat – delicious!

225ml (³/₄ cup plus 2 tbsp) water

2 tbsp yellow mustard seeds

165g (³/₄ cup) sugar

75ml (¹/₄ cup plus 1 tbsp) white wine or apple cider vinegar, normal strength

¹/₄ tsp white pepper

1 long cucumber

Finely chopped dill and parsley

Bring the water and mustard seeds to the boil, cook for 5 minutes. Add the sugar, vinegar and pepper, simmer until the sugar has dissolved. Set aside to cool.

Peel the cucumber and slice thinly, preferably using a mandolin slicer. Put the cucumber slices into a serving bowl with the chopped dill and parsley and cover with the lukewarm pickling liquid. Leave to infuse and cool for 10 minutes then refrigerate for a further 10 minutes.

Carrot and onion pickles

Lökinlagda morötter

This zesty carrot and onion pickle works equally well with barbecued meat – whether beef, lamb or pork – as it does with roast chicken, or rye bread topped with brie or camembert. As this version is cold pickled, it is very quick to make and is ready to eat after 12 hours. It will keep for several weeks in the fridge.

2 carrots

1 red/Spanish onion

60ml (¹/₄ cup) white or apple cider vinegar, normal strength

110g (¹/₂ cup) caster sugar

150ml (¹/₂ cup plus 1 tbsp) water

Peel and julienne the carrots. Halve the red onion and slice finely. Put the julienned carrot and sliced onion in a glass jar with a lid.

Combine the vinegar, sugar and water and stir until the sugar is completely dissolved. Cover the carrot and onion with the pickling liquid. It will be ready to eat after about 12 hours, and will keep in the fridge for 1–2 weeks.

Fermented red onion
Inlagd rödlök

This is a modern twist on the traditional pickled onion. For one it uses red (or Spanish) onion instead of the brown variety, and uses both herbs and citrus juices for an interesting and different take on the 'standard' pickled onion, making it sweeter and softer than the traditional version. It adds flavour and zest to any grilled meat, and is likely to become a 'must' to accompany your homemade hamburgers.

5 red/Spanish onions, peeled and thinly sliced

4 sprigs fresh thyme, optional

4 sprigs fresh rosemary

500ml (2 cups) lime or lemon juice

250ml (1 cup) apple cider or white vinegar, normal strength

1 tsp sea salt flakes

4 tbsp caster sugar

1 tbsp white peppercorns

Place the onion slices in a sterilised glass jar – push down and fill the jar to capacity. Slip the herb sprigs in along the side of the jar.

Combine the lime juice, vinegar, salt, sugar and peppercorns and stir until the salt and sugar have completely dissolved. Pour the pickling liquid over the onion, put the lid on tightly and rest for 24 hours.

After 24 hours, pour the liquid into a separate container, but do not discard. The onion has now softened and can easily be pressed down again and more freshly sliced red onion can be added. Push the onion down tightly to again fill the jar to capacity then add as much of the pickling liquid as will fit. Rest for another 24 hours. Repeat this process until you have the right quantity of pickled onion for your needs.

It will be ready to consume after 1 week from the first day of pickling. The lovely pinkish-red colour of the onion looks stunning on top of hamburgers, cheese sandwiches or alongside grilled steak. It will keep in the fridge for 2–3 weeks.

Old-fashioned 'jam' cucumber

Syltad gurka

As the name suggests, this is an old-fashioned version of the pickled cucumber. For starters, the peel and seeds are removed, and the pickling liquid is much sweeter, hence the name 'jam' cucumber. It is best served with meat casseroles, fried meat or as a topping on crisp bread with cheese or chicken liver pâté.

500ml (2 cups) water

50ml (¼ cup) apple cider vinegar, double strength

500g (2¼ cups) caster sugar

½ tbsp salt

1 cinnamon stick

20g/1 oz fresh ginger, sliced

2-3 long cucumbers

Mix the water, vinegar, sugar, salt, cinnamon stick and ginger in a stainless steel saucepan.

Peel the cucumber, cut in half lengthwise and remove the seeds. Cut into 5mm thick slices. Add the cucumber to the pickling liquid and bring to the boil then remove from the heat and stand aside to cool.

Pour the cucumber and liquid into glass pickling jars, close the lids tightly and put in the fridge. The jam cucumber will be ready after 3-4 days, and will keep for at least a month in the fridge.

Quick red onion pickles

Snabbinlagd rödlök

2 medium red/Spanish onions, peeled and thinly sliced

50ml (¼ cup) white wine or apple cider vinegar, normal strength

4 tbsp caster sugar

200ml (¾ cup plus 1 tbsp) water

¼ tsp sea salt

Put the red onion slices in a glass bowl. Combine the vinegar, sugar and water in a stainless steel saucepan and bring to the boil. Cover the onion with the pickling liquid then sprinkle over the sea salt. Set aside to cool in the fridge. The onion will be ready to eat after 12 hours, and will keep in the fridge for 1–2 weeks.

Pickled red cabbage
Inlagd rödkål

The colourful pickled red cabbage is particularly appreciated by the Danes, especially when served on top of their beloved pâté on rye open sandwich. In this recipe the cabbage stays crunchy; the red wine contributes to its luscious deep red colour and full flavour. It is excellent with roasts, cold cut meat, or added to a cabbage and carrot salad.

500g/1 lb red cabbage, finely shredded

25g (¼ cup) coarse sea salt

500ml (2 cups) apple cider vinegar, normal strength

300ml (1¼ cups) red wine

440g (2 cups) caster sugar

2 tsp white peppercorns

6 bay leaves

2 tbsp yellow mustard seeds

Put the shredded cabbage in a colander over a big bowl or the sink, sprinkle with salt and mix through the cabbage. Leave for 3 hours at room temperature then drain and rinse the salt off under cold running water. Pat dry with a clean tea towel.

Combine the vinegar, wine, sugar, peppercorns and bay leaves in a big stainless steel saucepan and simmer until the liquid has reduced by about half. The pickling liquid will now be quite sweet and sticky. Set aside for 10 minutes to infuse.

Strain the pickling liquid through a sieve into a bowl and discard peppercorns and bay leaves. Put the cabbage and mustard seeds into a sterilised glass jar, pour over the pickling liquid and seal tightly. The pickled red cabbage will be ready to eat after 1-2 days and will last for a month in the fridge.

Pickled beetroot

Inlagda röbetor

Making your own pickled beetroot is very easy, and you will be well rewarded with your efforts as homemade beetroot is way ahead of its canned cousin when it comes to taste, texture and nutrition. Do be sure to wear an apron though as it is virtually impossible to cook beetroot without some of the beautiful deep red juice splashing onto your clothes!

STEP 1 – BOILING

1kg/2 lb fresh beetroot

Water

STEP 2 - PICKLING

500ml (2 cups) liquid from step 1

165g (¾ cup) caster sugar

125ml (½ cup) apple cider vinegar, double strength

½ tsp white peppercorns

1 bay leaf

6 whole cloves

Clean the beetroot and remove the green part only, keeping the rest of the beetroot intact. Put in a saucepan and add enough water to cover. Bring to the boil and cook for 20–40 minutes or until the beetroot is tender. If sizes vary, remove the smaller beetroot when done and continue cooking the larger ones.

When soft, remove the beetroot from the pan and rinse under cold water but do not discard the boiling liquid. Remove the skin by rubbing the beetroot between your hands, or use a peeler – the peel will come off very easily. Cut the big beetroot into thick slices or quarters and put into sterilised glass jars with tight-fitting lids.

Measure 500ml (2 cups) of the water used for boiling the beetroot and put it through a muslin cloth or coffee filter to remove any impurities. Pour the beetroot water into a saucepan and add the sugar, vinegar, white peppercorns, bay leaf and cloves. Cover and bring to the boil then gently simmer for 3–4 minutes.

Pour the hot pickling liquid over the beetroots, ensuring they are completely covered. Put the lids on tightly and refrigerate. The beetroot is ready to eat after approximately 24 hours but will benefit from a longer infusion period. Keep the pickled beetroot in the fridge for up to 3 months.

BREAD

Rye bread with walnuts and apricots
Valnötsbröd

There is possibly nothing genuinely 'traditional' about this recipe, other than as long as I can remember my grandmother baked a fruit and walnut bread for special occasions. Walnuts and dried apricots were exotic and not readily available when grandmother first baked this loaf, hence she considered it a bread to be celebrated, not unceremoniously scoffed down by hungry grandchildren.

65g (½ cup) dried apricots

65g (½ cup) walnuts

65g (½ cup) golden linseeds

70g (½ cup) sunflower seeds

275g (2½ cups) wholemeal flour

300g (2½ cups) plain flour

1 tsp bicarbonate of soda

1 tsp baking powder

2 tsp salt

100ml (½ cup) dark syrup

1L (4 cups) buttermilk,
or unsweetened natural yoghurt

Preheat the oven to 175°C/350°F.

Chop the apricots and walnuts coarsely and mix with all dry ingredients in a bowl. Whisk the syrup and buttermilk or yoghurt in a separate bowl then add to the flour mixture. If the mix is very dry, add more buttermilk or yoghurt – the mix should be quite thick, yet moist.

Line a 2L (4 pints) baking tin with baking paper and add the batter. Bake in the middle of the oven for 50 minutes then remove the bread from the tin and bake it on the oven rack for another 10 minutes to create a nice crust.

Danish rye bread

Danskt rågbröd – Rugbrød (Danish)

The dark and sour Danish rye bread, rugbrød, is now famous the world over. It is extremely nutritious as it is low in fat, contains no oil or sugar and is very rich in whole grains and dietary fibre. The Danes have a saying that describes the only way to eat their beloved rugbrød - with 'enough butter to make an imprint of your teeth'.

This recipe is the complete opposite to the healthy no-knead bread earlier in this section, as you need plenty of time and dedication to make it, but after you've made it once, you're likely to make time to make it again and again. It also makes a perfect present for a bread-loving friend!

MAKING THE RYE BREAD SOURDOUGH STARTER (3-4 DAYS)

125g/4 oz rye flour

200ml (³/₄ cup plus 1 tbsp) water

Generous pinch of salt

1 tbsp honey

1 tbsp plain yoghurt

Mix all the ingredients in a bowl to form a mixture of almost mud-like consistency. Cover with plastic film, punching holes in the film to let it breathe. Leave to mature for 2 days. On the third day mix in some extra rye flour and water, leave until it starts bubbling (for another day or two). Once it is bubbling, it's ready to use. The sourdough starter will keep in the fridge for 2 weeks.

MAKING THE RUGBRØD (2-3 DAYS)

Day 1

250g/9 oz sourdough starter

125g/4 oz whole rye grains

25g/1 oz linseed

75g/2.6 oz wheat flour

250ml (1 cup) lukewarm water

¹/₂ tbsp salt

³/₄ tbsp honey

On day 1, stir the first-day ingredients together, leave overnight under a wet cloth. Check to make sure the dough does not get too dry; if it does, spray with a little water.

Day 2

550g/1.2 lb rye flour

¹/₂ tbsp salt

³/₄ tbsp honey

450ml (1³/₄ cup plus 1 tbsp) water

Preheat the oven to 170°C/350°F.

On day 2, take the day 1 dough and knead together with day 2 ingredients for 10 minutes. Take away 250g/9 oz of sourdough for next time you're baking, put in a plastic container in the fridge. (This way your next rye bread will only take two days to make!)

Oil a large bread loaf tin. Pour in the dough - it should be the consistency of heavy mud. Leave to rise for 4–6 hours (it won't rise more than a few centimetres/ an inch) and bake at 170°C/350°F for 1 hour and 45 minutes. Take the rye bread out of the tin, put on an oven rack and bake for another 15 minutes.

When done, carefully remove from the oven and place on a rack to cool. When the bread is still slightly warm, wrap it in a clean kitchen towel and put in a plastic bag – this will help to soften the crust which can be hard to cut otherwise. Leave to cool completely under a kitchen towel if you prefer the crust to remain hard.

Wait until the next day before cutting into thin slices of approx 5-8mm thickness.

SPICES USED IN SWEDISH BAKING AND COOKING

When grouping together the spices used in Swedish cooking you get the sense they depict those used in Middle Eastern cooking. But luckily the spice trade made its way to Scandinavia a long, long time ago, and those exotic flavourings were readily incorporated into everyday baking and cooking. These are the spices used all year round in many different ways – then there are spices such as saffron, primarily used in buns (*lussekatter*) eaten on December 13 every year to celebrate Lucia, the bringer of light.

Baking dish arrangement – top to bottom / left to right
Row 1: Ginger, cloves, whole white pepper, caraway seed
Row 2: Cardamon pods, cumin seed, allspice/pimento, aniseed stars
Row 3: Ground cinnamon, dried thyme, mustard seed, fennel seed

Healthy no knead bread
Röra-ihop bröd i långpanna

This easy-to-make bread is not only delicious it is also very healthy to boot, and when in the oven the spices (preferably freshly ground) fill the kitchen with a beautiful aroma. There is no need to leave the dough to prove, then knead, then prove again — just mix all the ingredients and put into the baking dish. It also freezes really well, and is scrumptious toasted. So what's not to like?

2 tsp caraway seeds

2 tsp fennel seeds

2 tsp aniseeds

300g (2½ cups) white flour

75g (¾ cup) rolled oats

90g (¾ cup) wholemeal flour

165g (1½ cups) rye flour

85g (½ cup) linseeds

70g (½ cup) pumpkin seeds

70g (½ cup) sunflower seeds

2 tsp salt

2 tsp bicarbonate of soda

2 tsp baking powder

1-1.2L (4–4¾ cups) buttermilk*

100ml (1.3 cup plus 1 tbsp) golden syrup

(*) If buttermilk is not available, substitute for soured milk or unsweetened natural yoghurt mixed with milk to make up the required volume of liquid.

Preheat the oven to 175°C/350°F.

Line a rectangular baking dish, 25 x 30cm/10 x 12 inches, with baking paper and grease with butter – the inclusion of syrup can make the bread stick to the baking paper.

Dry roast the caraway and fennel seeds, set aside to cool then grind with the aniseeds to a flour-like consistency. Blend all dry ingredients in a large bowl. In a separate bowl mix 1L (4 cups) of the buttermilk and the golden syrup then combine with the dry mixture. The mixture will be quite solid and sticky, add the rest of the buttermilk if too dry.

Bake in the middle of the oven for 1 hour. Check with a metal skewer to see if it is cooked through, if it's still wet then leave in the oven for another 5 minutes or until done.

When ready, allow to cool on a rack before cutting into squares.

NOTE: This bread gets a really hard crust, which is great if you like crusty bread. If you don't, simply put the bread into a plastic snap-lock bag once the bread has cooled for a minute or so – this will soften the crust.

Crispbread with seeds
Knäckebröd med frön

This wonderful crisp bread is very nutritious and rich in fibre, and with this easy recipe you will whip some up in no time. Crisp bread figures heavily in the Swedish diet whether for breakfast, lunch or dinner. This recipe takes less than 30 minutes to make and is well worth the effort. The classic topping for any crisp bread is cheese, such as Jarlsberg, Spiced Gouda or Danish Blue. Other popular toppings are smoked sausage (such as Mettwurst) with tomato, pâté with pickled cucumber – and last but not least salty, creamed cod roe topped with slices of hard-boiled eggs. That last topping, however, may take a while for a non-Swede to appreciate . . .

55g (½ cup) rye flour

55g (½ cup) wholemeal flour

35g (¼ cup) sunflower seeds

35g (¼ cup) pumpkin seeds

35g (¼ cup) sesame seeds

40g (¼ cup) golden linseeds

½ tsp sea salt flakes

50ml (¼ cup) canola oil

200ml (¾ cup plus 1 tbsp) boiling water

Preheat the oven to 150°C/300°F.

Place all the dry ingredients into a bowl and mix. Add the canola oil and mix through then add the boiling water and combine. Spread the mix out on a piece of baking paper, put another piece of baking paper on top and use a rolling pin to flatten until the mixture is around 3mm thick – don't make it too thin as the crisp bread will then be brittle and burn more easily.

Remove the top piece of baking paper and place the crisp bread in the middle of the oven and bake for 30–35 minutes – it should be quite hard and crispy when done. Break into pieces when cool and store in an airtight container.

Cold-proven breakfast rolls

Kalljästa frukostbullar

I'm not exactly sure how to translate the name of these wonderful breakfast rolls where the dough is prepared at night then left to rise in the fridge overnight! This recipe makes about ten breakfast rolls, satisfyingly filling, yet soft with a crunchy crust. Add to this the aroma of freshly baked bread and you are on your way to a very harmonious start to the day.

MAKES 8-10 ROLLS

20g/1 oz fresh yeast

200ml (³/₄ cup plus 1 tbsp) cold water

1 tbsp canola oil

¹/₂ tsp salt flakes

90g (³/₄ cup) wholemeal flour

140g (1¹/₄ cups) plain flour

Break up the yeast in a bowl. Add a little of the cold water and stir until combined.

Add the rest of the water, oil, salt and flours. Work the mixture into a smooth dough, either by hand or in a mixer until the dough lifts from the sides of the mixing bowl. Add some flour on a clean bench and divide into 8-10 portions. Shape into round buns and put on an oven tray lined with baking paper. Cover with a clean tea towel and leave to prove in the fridge overnight.

Preheat the oven to 250°C/500°F.

Remove the tray from the fridge and let stand for 30 minutes at room temperature. (If you want to speed up the final rising process place the tray in a cold oven with a dish of boiling water at the base for about 10 minutes.)

Brush the rolls with cold water and sprinkle with your choice of topping – sesame seeds, linseeds, pumpkin or sunflower seeds, or perhaps some grated cheese.

Bake in the oven for around 10 minutes and allow to cool on a rack before serving with your favourite condiments.

BUNS & CAKES

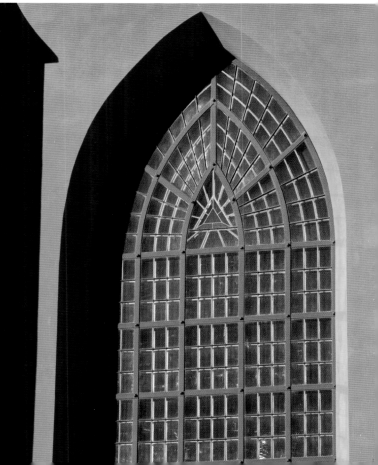

Cinnamon buns

Kanelbullar

It may be that the only Swedish cinnamon buns you've ever tasted are those in an IKEA restaurant. As good as the IKEA buns are they just don't compare to a soft and sweet cinnamon bun straight from the oven. One of the best ways to enjoy the fresher-than-fresh bun is with a large, cold glass of milk — sounds odd, but it definitely works so do try it!

Each year on October 4, the Swedes celebrate Kanelbullens Dag — Cinnamon Bun Day. This recent "tradition" was started in 1999 by Hembakningsrådet — Homebaking Adviser — to promote Sweden's most loved bun, and of course with a view to increasing sales of yeast, sugar and flour. These days, more than 8 million cinnamon buns are sold on the Kanelbullens Dag in Sweden.

You do have to love the Swedes' love of traditions, big and small, ancient and recent, don't you?

MAKES APPROXIMATELY 20 BUNS

DOUGH

50g/2 oz fresh or 7g/¼ oz dry yeast

300ml (1¼ cups) full cream milk

55g (¼ cup) sugar

½ tsp salt

1 tsp cardamom, freshly ground

500g (3¼ cups) plain flour

50g/2 oz soft butter

FILLING

75g/2.6 oz butter

55g (¼ cup) sugar

3 tsp cinnamon

TOPPING

1 egg

1 tbsp water

Pearl sugar or crushed sugar cubes

Crumble the fresh yeast into a bowl, or add the dry yeast. Gently heat the milk in a saucepan until it reaches 37°C/100°F or 'finger' temperature. Pour a small amount of the milk over the yeast and stir until the yeast has dissolved.

Add the remaining milk, sugar, salt, cardamom and most of the flour (save a small amount for rolling the dough out on) and stir together to make a soft dough, then add the soft butter cut into small cubes.

Check the consistency - the dough should be quite soft before the first proving, so the trick is to knead it for a long time – up to 10 minutes if using a mixer. If kneading by hand, this may take even longer – the important thing is that the dough should still be soft.

When done, put the dough back in a lightly oiled bowl (or leave in the machine bowl) and cover with a clean tea towel to rise in a warm and draught-free place for 30–60 minutes.

While the dough is rising, mix the ingredients for the filling until soft and easy to spread.

On a lightly floured surface, roll the dough out to a rectangle roughly 30x40cm/12x16 inches. Spread the filling across the dough and starting from one of the long edges, roll it up. Position it on its seam and cut into 2.5cm/1 inch thick slices.

Put the slices into paper patty pans, cut edge facing up. Set aside to prove under a tea towel for another 30 minutes, or until they spring back when prodded.

Preheat the oven to 250°C/500°F.

Brush the rolls with the egg wash, sprinkle with pearl sugar and/or flaked almonds and bake in the middle of the oven for about 8-10 minutes.

TIPS FOR THE SOFTEST AND TASTIEST CINNAMON BUNS

❀ For the softest and tastiest buns use premium cake flour. Bread flour will also work but the buns will be denser.

❀ Put the dough to prove in a cold oven with a bowl of hot water at the base – it provides a perfect even temperature and is draught free.

❀ Do not rush the proving of the dough - allow it to take the time it needs to rise even if longer than stipulated in the recipe.

❀ Adding a couple of ice cubes on the baking tray helps make the buns nice and moist.

ALTERNATIVE FILLINGS
❀ Ground cardamom instead of cinnamon
❀ Vanilla sugar
❀ Raspberries and shredded coconut

Waffles

Våfflor

Waffles are one of those comfort foods that will always be a hit with young and old alike. In Sweden waffles even have their own name day – Våffel Dagen (Waffel Day) on March 23 each year – bringing together that irresistible urge to celebrate old traditions while simultaneously enjoying some seriously indulgent food. This recipe makes very light and crispy waffles.

MAKES 8–10 WAFFLES

285g (2 ½ cups plus 1 tbsp) plain flour

2 tsp baking powder

200ml (¾ cup plus 1 tbsp) milk

200ml (¾ cup plus 1 tbsp) thick cream

2 eggs

75g/2.6 oz butter

Sift the flour and baking powder and combine. In a separate bowl whisk together the milk, cream and eggs. Gently combine the flour with the egg and milk mixture and stir until smooth (the mixture will be quite thick). Rest for 15 minutes then melt the butter and add to the waffle mixture when cooled.

Heat the waffle iron and grease with butter for the first waffle only. Pour approximately 50ml (¼ cup) of the mixture into each waffle mould, close the lid and bake until golden, approximately 3–4 minutes.

Traditionally the waffles are served with whipped cream and strawberry or raspberry jam. Or for a healthier option serve with yoghurt and fresh berries or fruit.

You can also stray from the sweet option altogether by adding a savoury topping, such as smoked salmon and crème fraîche and garnish with dill and lemon. This savoury version is perfect to serve as an elegant and tasty entrée dish as well.

Strawberry and cream cake
Jordgubbstårta

Nothing says summer to a Swede more than strawberries and nothing says Midsummer more than 'jordgubbstårta'. It is a given on every Midsummer smorgasbord and there would be few, if any, summer festivities where this cake does not take pride of place on the dessert table. It is light, it is fresh, and uses a simple sponge cake as a base, filled with vanilla custard, cream and strawberries and then decorated with lots and lots of fresh strawberries.

SERVES 8–10

SPONGE CAKE

150g/5 oz butter

165g (³/₄ cup) caster sugar

3 eggs

140g (1¹/₄ cups) flour

2 tsp baking powder

2 tsp vanilla sugar

CUSTARD FILLING

100ml (¹/₃ cup plus 1 tbsp) cream

100ml (¹/₃ cup plus 1 tbsp) full cream milk

2 egg yolks

2 tsp corn flour

1 tsp sugar

¹/₂ vanilla bean

STRAWBERRY CREAM FILLING

330g (2 cups) strawberries

100ml (¹/₃ cup plus 1 tbsp) thick cream

TOPPING

200-300ml (³/₄ – 1¹/₄ cups) thick cream

55g (¹/₄ cup) sugar

1 tsp vanilla sugar

660g (4 cups) fresh strawberries

SPONGE CAKE
Preheat the oven to 175°C/350°F.

Grease and crumb a round baking dish, approx 25cm/10 inches in diameter.

Beat the butter and sugar until white and fluffy. Add one egg at a time and beat vigorously. Mix the flour, baking powder and vanilla sugar in a separate bowl. Fold the flour mix into the egg, butter and sugar mixture and pour into the baking dish.

Bake for about 40 minutes. Leave the sponge cake to cool in the dish for a couple of minutes, then tip onto the serving platter or cake stand.

VANILLA CUSTARD
Whisk together the cream, milk, egg yolks, corn flour and sugar in a stainless steel saucepan. Scrape the seeds from the vanilla bean and add both seeds and the bean to the custard mix.

Gently heat the custard over moderate heat until it starts simmering (be careful not to boil it). When the custard has thickened, remove from the heat and place the saucepan into iced water in the sink to prevent it from curdling.

STRAWBERRY AND CREAM FILLING
Rinse and clean the strawberries for the filling, draining away any excess water. Mash with a fork. Whip the cream and vanilla sugar until thick and firm then gently fold in the strawberry mash.

ASSEMBLE THE CAKE
Cut the cake into three rounds.

Spread the custard on the base round and place the second round on top. Spread the strawberry and cream filling on the second round. Place the third round on top.

Whip the cream for the topping, along with the sugar and vanilla sugar. Spread it all around the cake and garnish with strawberries – either whole, halved or sliced as per your preference. You can also add grated chocolate on top and toasted almond flakes around the sides for a more elegant presentation.

Tosca cake

Tosca kaka

This is yet another seriously addictive cake and one of Sweden's most loved — the soft and moist cake topped with the crunchy almond topping is more moreish than many more elaborate creations. And once you've become truly addicted, you may even double the quantity for the Tosca mix for an even crunchier taste experience.

SERVES 8-10

CAKE MIX

100g/3.5 oz butter

125g (1 cup) plain flour

1½ tsp baking powder

1½ tsp vanilla sugar

3 eggs

165g (¾ cup) caster sugar

TOSCA TOPPING

100g/3.5 oz flaked almonds

65g (¼ cup plus 2 tsp) caster sugar

50g/2 oz butter

1 tbsp plain flour

2 tbsp cream

Preheat the oven to 175°C/350°F.

Grease and crumb a round springform cake tin, approximately 24cm/9 inches in diameter.

Melt the butter over low heat and set aside to cool. Sift the flour, baking powder and vanilla sugar together. In a separate bowl, beat the eggs and sugar until white and fluffy then gently fold in the flour mix and stir until smooth, followed by the melted butter.

Pour the batter into the tin and bake for 20–25 minutes or until almost done, the cake should still be 'wet' in the centre.

Towards the end of the 20–25 minutes, put all the ingredients for the Tosca topping in a saucepan and stir continuously while gently bringing to the boil.

Remove the almost-done cake from the oven and spread the topping over it. Increase the temperature to 225°C/450°F, return the cake to the oven and bake for another 8-10 minutes, or until the Tosca topping is golden and slightly caramelised. Keep an eye on the cake as the Tosca mix can burn very quickly due to the high sugar content.

When cooked through, leave the cake to cool on the benchtop and for the Tosca mix to harden before removing from the tin.

The Tosca cake is usually served without embellishments – it is that good – but of course it can also be served with a dollop of cream or ice cream if you wish.

Swedish sticky chocolate cake (aka Gooey cake)

Kladdkaka

Kladdkaka is such an institution on the Swedish culinary consciousness that is needs no further description than simply 'Gooey cake'. One of the favourite sweets, whether served as a decadent dessert or with a cup of coffee at 'fika' time. It is gooey, sticky and chocolatey, but not overly sweet. There is only one way to serve this delicacy — with lots of vanilla-flavoured whipped cream and perhaps a couple of berries (mainly for show!).

The kladdkaka can either be served lukewarm when it is at its most gooey or cold when it is chewier and perhaps has a little more flavour. Either way, the whipped cream is a must.

There is an absolute plethora of recipes for kladdkaka, and this is the recipe my family uses. The inclusion of dark chocolate makes it even more gooey, and substituting some of the butter with a little cooking oil makes the cake extra crunchy yet chewy on top! So what's not to like I ask you, especially as it is so easy to make.

You can use the cocoa powder found in most supermarkets, but raw cacao is better as it is unprocessed and gives the cake a deeper chocolate flavour.

SERVES 8–10

50g/2 oz butter

3 tbsp cooking oil (preferably canola oil)

130g (½ cup plus 1 tbsp) caster sugar

2 large or 3 small eggs

135g (½ cup plus 1 tbsp) brown sugar

125g (1 cup) plain flour

4 tbsp raw cacao

2 tsp baking powder

2 tsp vanilla sugar

70g/2.5 oz 70% dark chocolate

Preheat the oven to 150°C/300°F.

Grease a round springform cake tin approximately 24cm/9 inches in diameter. Dust lightly with flour.

Melt the butter and set aside to cool then add the oil.

In a bowl whisk together the sugar and eggs until very soft and fluffy, then add the butter and oil mix. In another bowl mix all the dry ingredients. Chop the dark chocolate into approx 10mm pieces and add to the dry ingredients.

Gently fold the flour mix into the egg and butter batter. Pour into the cake tin and bake in the middle of the oven for 30 minutes. Check with a skewer to see if the cake it cooked – the cake should still be sticky in the centre but set around the edges. It will seem far too uncooked at this stage, but the centre will stabilise once cool.

Cool the cake in the tin for around 20 minutes – it is likely to collapse in the centre during this time, so don't worry. Run a knife around the edge of the tin to loosen the cake and put it on a serving platter.

To serve, dust with icing sugar and a healthy dollop of vanilla-infused whipped cream.

Mazarin cakes
Mazariner

This is another old recipe dating back several centuries. The Mazarin is believed to be named after Cardinal Mazarin, who ruled France alongside King Louis XIV in the 17th Century. Whatever its origin, it is an elegant small cake with a marzipan-like filling. For best results, use foil patty pans, or if using paper pans, use two for each mazarin. The cakes depicted have been baked in much loved old-fashioned steel baking patties handed down from my mother.

MAKES 12–14 CAKES

PASTRY

100g/3.5 oz butter, at room temperature

55g (½ cup) icing sugar

1 large egg yolk

95g (¾ cup) plain flour

ALMOND FILLING

120g/4 oz almonds

85g/3 oz butter

80g (¾ cup) icing sugar

2 large eggs

GLAZE

55g (½ cup) icing sugar

1 tbsp water

Preheat the oven to 175°C/350°F.

The pastry: With an electric beater, mix the butter and sugar until the sugar is completely dissolved. Add the egg yolk, mix, and then quickly fold in the flour. Put in the fridge to rest for 20–30 minutes, this will make the pastry easier to handle.

Almond filling: Blanch the almonds in water over low heat for two to three minutes. Put almonds in a clean, dry kitchen towel and rub to remove the skins, they will come away easily. In a food processor grind the almonds into a flour-like consistency. In a separate bowl, beat the butter and sugar until white and fluffy. Add the almond flour and eggs and mix thoroughly.

Grease the Mazarin patty pans. Roll out the pastry to about 2mm thickness. Line each patty pan with the pastry, smoothing out with your thumbs. Spoon the almond filling into the pastry-lined pans and bake in the middle of the oven for 25 minutes.

Leave the Mazarins to cool on a rack. Mix the icing sugar and water for the glaze and either brush or pour it over the Mazarins when completely cold.

DRINKS

Iced berry tea
Iste med bär

On a hot summer day, iced tea is one of the most thirst-quenching drinks you can have. It is also one of the easiest summer drinks to make using ingredients usually found in the cupboard. This iced tea bursts with flavour and the sweet berries reduce the need for sugar — making this iced tea very healthy and nutritious indeed. The tea also takes on a wonderful and rich colour best displayed in a glass jug.

4-6 berry flavoured teabags

800ml (3³/₄ cups) hot water

750ml (3 cups) mineral water

40g (¹/₄ cup) frozen raspberries

40g (¹/₄ cup) frozen blueberries

40g (¹/₄ cup) frozen strawberries

Steep the teabags in simmering water for about 15 minutes to make a very strong brew. Remove from the heat and set aside to cool then put in the fridge to chill completely.

When ready to serve, remove the tea bags and add mineral water and the frozen berries. Serve in tall glasses, and garnish with strawberry, mint or for extra colour a slice of lemon. Serve with sugar on the side for the sweet-tooths of the family.

Rhubarb and vanilla drink

Rabarber dricka

I first tasted this drink a few years ago when visiting family and friends in Sweden. My cousin had caught one of the breakfast TV shows and thought this recipe sounded delicious. Well, he was right — it is very refreshing with the vanilla bean softening the tart taste of the rhubarb. It is also well suited to have some vodka or gin added if your preference is for a drink with a bit of 'punch'.

MAKES 1.5L

10 stalks of ripe rhubarb

330g (1½ cups) sugar

1.4L (5½ cups) water

½ vanilla pod

6 frozen strawberries

Fresh strawberries, mint or lime slices

Wash the rhubarb and cut into 2–3cm/1 inch pieces. Cut the vanilla bean lengthwise. Put the rhubarb, sugar, water and the vanilla bean in a stainless steel saucepan. Bring to the boil and cook on medium-high for 5 minutes.

Remove from the heat and add the frozen strawberries. Set aside to infuse for at least 2 hours then put through a fine sieve to drain the juice – without pressing or squeezing the rhubarb and strawberry pulp. This will result in a clear, smooth and full-flavoured juice.

Chill and pour into pre-chilled glasses. Garnish with strawberries, mint or lime slices.

Strawberry and melon drink

Jordgubb och melon dricka

SERVES 4-6

200g/7 oz fresh or frozen strawberries

200g/7 oz watermelon, honey dew or cantaloupe

300ml (1¼ cups) water

2 tbsp sugar or honey (if requiring sweetening)

Mash the strawberries with a hand blender or in a mixer until the strawberries are completely juiced. Peel the melon and cut into small cubes and add to the strawberry mash, mix until the juice is smooth. Taste for sweetness and add sugar or honey if not sufficiently sweet.

To serve, dip the glasses in a shallow dish with a little water then into another dish with sugar, to form a sugar-crust around the rim of the glass. Or garnish with a slice of lime and/or strawberry and lemon balm.

Mixed berry cordial

Blandbärssaft

The great thing about this cordial is that it is so full of flavour it is unlikely to last very long — and as long as it's consumed within a couple of weeks it doesn't require preservatives or additives. Use whatever berries are in season, or use frozen berries — mix and match to suit your own taste buds. I like my mixed berry cordial made with lots of blueberries, blackberries, raspberries and a few strawberries for extra sweetness. This results in a dark cordial, which when mixed with water or mineral water is a vibrant dark red colour.

2kg (12 cups) mixed berries (raspberries, strawberries, blackberries, black or red currants)

1L (4 cups) water

550g (2½ cups) sugar

Clean and rinse the berries, taking care all stalks, grit or impurities are removed. Put the berries into a saucepan, add the water, cover and bring to the boil then reduce the heat to a simmer for about 10 minutes. Using a wooden spoon, squeeze the berries against the sides of the pan to extract the berry juices.

Pour the berries and juice into a muslin cloth lined sieve – draining all liquid out of the berry pulp will take some time and may even be best left overnight. For a clear and smooth cordial, do not push the pulp through the sieve as this may squeeze through minute fruit solids which could ferment and alter the cordial properties.

When all the berry juices have drained from the pulp, pour into a saucepan and bring to the boil. Reduce the heat, add half the sugar and stir until it has completely dissolved, taste for sweetness and then add more sugar as required, stir until completely dissolved. Bring the cordial back to the boil. Take the pan off the heat and remove any froth that has formed on the surface. Pour the cordial into sterilised warm bottles, seal and set aside to cool. Store the cordial bottles in the fridge.

> **TIPS:** For cordial that will be consumed within two weeks of making, there is no need to add preservatives. If you know it will last for longer than that, you can either pour the cordial into clean, warm plastic bottles and put in the freezer or add preservatives (i.e. sodium benzoate or citric acid) as recommended on the package.

SMOOTHIES

Smoothies have become very popular the world over for their creamy and smooth texture, sweetness and versatility. Although not traditional to the Swedish cuisine, these recipes use traditional taste combinations – redcurrants, and apple and cinnamon. The coffee smoothie is included because it is simply too delicious to leave out!

The best smoothies are made from fresh berries and/or fruit, but out of season frozen berries are an excellent substitute.

Redcurrant smoothie

Röda vinbärssmoothie

Redcurrants are not as sweet as the more popular 'smoothie' berries such as strawberries, blueberries and raspberries. Combining the redcurrants with a ripe banana overcomes this 'shortcoming' however and the outcome is very refreshing – tangy and sweet at the same time. And of course healthy and nutritious!

MAKES 1 LARGE OR 2 SMALL GLASSES

500g/1 lb fresh redcurrants

2 small bananas, or other sweet and soft-fleshed fruit such as mango, peach or nectarine

150ml (1/2 cup plus 1 tbsp) cranberry or blackcurrant cordial

500ml (2 cups) plain yoghurt

Honey or sugar (optional)

Ice cubes

Rinse and clean the redcurrants by removing the stalks – put a few berries aside for garnish. Mash the redcurrants and banana with a hand blender or in a mixer until smooth then add the cordial and yoghurt and blend on high until smooth. Taste and if desired add honey or sugar.

Pour into a glass and garnish with the remaining redcurrants. For a very cold smoothie add a few ice cubes to the glass, top up with the smoothie and garnish with redcurrants.

Apple and cinnamon smoothie

Äpple och kanel smoothie

Continuing the Swedes' love affair with apple and cinnamon, this smoothie is not only quick and simple to make, it is also nutritious and very tasty. It is suitable for any time of the day – breakfast, lunch or just as a mid-afternoon snack. Once you've tried it, you're very likely to make it again and again – it is always very satisfying and addictively delicious!

MAKES 1 LARGE OR 2 SMALL GLASSES

1 apple, skin on, cubed

1/2 tsp cinnamon

1 tsp vanilla sugar

300ml (1 1/4 cups) plain yoghurt

For this recipe, choose an apple that is sweet and with a flesh that is a little soft. Rinse the apple, remove the core but keep the skin on and cut into small cubes. Place the apple cubes, cinnamon, vanilla sugar and half of the yoghurt in a mixer, or in a bowl if using a hand blender – mix until smooth then add the remainder of the yoghurt.

Pour into a glass and sprinkle a little cinnamon on top. For a very cold smoothie, add a few ice cubes to the glass, top up with the smoothie, and sprinkle with a little cinnamon.

Coffee smoothie
Kaffe smoothie

Admittedly there is nothing specifically Swedish or traditional about this smoothie, but given Swedes' love of coffee it does have a place in this publication. It's great as a breakfast on the run or as a mid-morning or mid-afternoon snack — and better for you than biscuits or chips.

MAKES 1 GLASS

1 banana

60ml (¼ cup) cold espresso or very strong brewed coffee

200ml (¾ cup plus 1 tbsp) plain yoghurt

Cinnamon

Peel and chop the banana, add to a blender or jug with the coffee and yoghurt and mix until smooth using a hand blender or mixer.

Pour into a pre-chilled glass and sprinkle with cinnamon.

RECIPE INDEX